LEADERSHIP—LOVE IT OR LEAVE IT

— ANGIE NOEL —

LEADERSHIP LOVE IT OR *LEAVE IT*

CHOOSING FOR YOURSELF
WHEN THE WORLD SAYS CLIMB

COPYRIGHT © 2019 ANGIE NOEL

All rights reserved.

LEADERSHIP—LOVE IT OR LEAVE IT
Choosing for Yourself When the World Says Climb

ISBN 978-1-5445-1307-2 *Paperback*
      978-1-5445-1306-5 *Ebook*

This book and every decent thing I may ever do with the rest of my life is dedicated to B. The absolute greatest joy of my life, you make every single thing more beautiful...even work!

CONTENTS

INTRODUCTION 9

1. HUMAN SUFFERING…AT WORK 21
2. THIS AIN'T YOUR GRANDPA'S LEADERSHIP 53
3. LEADING ON PURPOSE 73
4. YOUR LEADERSHIP, YOUR CONTEXT 93
5. OWN YOUR OWN SHIFT 115
6. LOVING LEADERSHIP IN ACTION 139

CONCLUSION 163

ACKNOWLEDGMENTS 169

ABOUT THE AUTHOR 173

INTRODUCTION

I sat in my car, staring at myself in the flip-down mirror, putting on my lipstick...stalling. I prayed, *God, please give me a reason not to go in. I mean, not a call from daycare or anything, but I could handle a small stomach virus if it would keep me from having to go in there today.* My stomach *was* gurgling, but that was pretty normal for this time of day. It always started as soon as I pulled into the parking garage. The sunshine immediately turned to darkness; the flickering fluorescents seemed to be guiding me straight to hell. My gut wrenched more and more with each level I circled until I finally parked on the roof. Daylight.

I sat there, still staring at myself in the mirror. *What is wrong with me?* I wondered. *This isn't me at all.* At least not the me I was just a few years earlier. And definitely not the me I wanted to be.

I felt lost and confused. How did I end up twenty pounds underweight? Why was I so irritable? Where did these heart palpitations and anxiety attacks come from, and why couldn't I get a full night's sleep? People close to me tried to blame my symptoms on new parenthood—I was the mother of a two-year-old—but this was more than parenting fatigue. My doctor's diagnosis wasn't much more helpful—she said it was "stress." I knew it wasn't just stress, either. I was suffering, physically and emotionally, and deep down, I knew work was to blame.

That's not how this was supposed to go. Work had always been important to me—I came from very humble beginnings, and working meant money in the bank, so I worked hard. From my first job at twelve, cleaning Mrs. Rothering's house down the street, to serving up fries at McDonald's, to working in some very prestigious healthcare systems, I was always striving to move up. A huge part of my identity was wrapped up in what I did for a living; it defined me. For much of my life, work *was* my life. But lately, I didn't even know who I was.

I had built a twenty-year career in human resources, and I was an HR leader in healthcare—a dream job. I had wanted to be "a leader" since I was a young girl, and I had a real passion for helping people; healthcare human resources seemed like a perfect fit. I had a six-figure salary, a nice office, a great support team, and plenty of challenging work. I had everything I could want. And I was miserable.

I hadn't always been this way. At one time, I approached work with enthusiasm, positivity, and a sense of urgency. I always wanted to do more. Lately, though, it was a struggle just finding the motivation to physically show up every day. I tried desperately to start fresh each day and reconnect to the joy I once had at work. I couldn't do it. It was painful. I felt isolated and, honestly, a little crazy, because I didn't understand what was happening to me.

The irony was that, working in HR, I'd heard the same story from countless leaders who had come to my office over the years. They were stressed out, exhausted, feeling overwhelmed, and struggling to figure out what the hell was happening to them.

Staring at my reflection in the car mirror, it hit me—I had become one of *them*. My heart sank. *So this is what disengagement feels like.* I thought about all of the people that I had listened to and coached over the years and realized I hadn't fully appreciated what they were experiencing until now. They weren't just leaders struggling to manage an ever-growing workload; they were disheartened, disconnected, and disengaged human beings. The more I reflected on my own suffering and the suffering of all those other people, the more angry I became. That wasn't how people were supposed to feel at work, especially leaders. Something had to change.

That realization, along with the need to alleviate my own suffering, led me to research the causes. What drove employees—and leaders—to disengage this way? With twenty years of HR experience under my belt, I knew a lot about "employee engagement." I had been through every exercise around—the annual surveys, the push for higher engagement "scores," and the never-ending action plans that are par for the course at most companies. But we never really talked about *disengagement*. When we did, the discussion was typically limited to tactics for moving the disengaged "numbers" either into the engaged column or out of the organization. It wasn't really about the people involved.

As I dove into the research, three things became clear. First, there was very little information out there about disengagement—why it's so prevalent, its impact on the people who experience it, and how to address it. Second, leaders get most, if not all, of the blame for disengagement. And third, leaders are not only being held responsible for disengagement—they're actually experiencing and suffering the symptoms of it just as much as their employees are.

The more I learned about disengagement and the ways

it is connected to leadership, the more frustrated I got. Something had to change; I suspected that that change would need to start with the leaders themselves.

Frankly, I was pissed—pissed enough to spend a year of my life writing this book for you.

* * *

When it comes to leadership, we tend to hear the same advice and platitudes over and over again, whether it's coming from leadership "experts," retired corporate bigwigs, or school teachers:

"There's a leader in every one of us."

"Be a leader, not a follower."

"Soar like an eagle or scratch the ground like a chicken."

"It's better to be the lion than the sheep."

The underlying assumption is that we should *all* be leaders—that every one of us should strive for roles with more responsibility and power, and that success is found at the top. School teachers say it, leadership "experts" say it, corporate bigwigs say it. Surely, it must be true.

As we say in Texas, I call bullshit.

Leadership is hard and complex. It can't be boiled down to "five essential qualities." And leadership is most definitely *not* for everyone.

Why do I say this? Because my experience and extensive research into leadership and engagement have left me one hundred percent convinced that if you don't fully appreciate, embrace, and—dare I say—*love* the responsibility of influencing and impacting other human beings, then you're creating suffering.

I know this sounds extreme in a culture where leadership *is* the goal. But think about all of the jobs you've ever had. What made the best job so great? Maybe it paid really well or maybe you got to do something you really enjoyed, but I'd be willing to bet you also had a good boss. Someone who inspired you in some way. Now think of your worst work experience. Did it happen to involve a bad boss? Was he a narcissist, a jerk, or maybe a really nice person who couldn't communicate clearly to save his life? Someone who should *not* have been leading people maybe? You're probably getting a little nauseated reliving that horror story right now. If you don't have such a tale on your resume, then you are one of the lucky few. According to several surveys, 50 percent to 75 percent of all employees have quit at least one job to escape a bad manager.

"Bad" leaders aren't necessarily bad people. You may even have known someone in a leadership position who seemed truly overwhelmed, stressed out, or flat-out unhappy in their role—this is a red flag that they may very well have been disengaged themselves. When "up" seems like the only way to success, people can sometimes find themselves in positions that exceed their competence or don't align with personal goals, or both. And leaders who don't know *why* they've taken on a leadership role tend to suffer or, at the very least, struggle. At the end of the day, suffering leaders *cannot* help others. Instead, they unintentionally spread their misery like a bad cold. What happens at the office rarely stays at the office. Instead, the stress from leadership that rubs off on employees also tends to follow those employees home, where they infect everyone around them—significant others, children, friends, and anyone else they interact with.

To create suffering in the workplace is to create suffering in employees' personal *and* professional lives. Suffering that leaves them feeling disconnected and disengaged from everything, including the very work that leaders are supposed to support them in doing.

This is why it's so critical to decide if leadership is really the right choice for you. A good leader—a professionally and personally fulfilled human being—can make even the most challenging work meaningful and have a positive impact on all aspects of an employee's life.

A good leader can break the cycle of disengagement. This is what *Leadership—Love It or Leave It* is all about.

A NEW REALITY

Everything about work is changing and fast. Technology and generational diversity, among other influences, are challenging every business in every industry to rethink how work gets done, where it's done, and who's doing it. Leadership, as a whole, is being pressured to evolve under increasingly intense and rapidly changing circumstances. And the change is happening—almost in spite of the multi-billion dollar leadership training industry struggling to keep up.

As traditional organizational structures of top-down control are beginning to give way to more transparent, collaborative, and networked models, a redistribution of authority is occurring. Leaders today face challenges that didn't even exist ten or fifteen years ago as followership has become more prevalent and social media more influential. With thumbs up or down, likes, hearts, and angry emojis, employees are increasingly expressing their love and frustration alike with the world on any number of public forums, such as Facebook, Instagram, and Glassdoor. They can also share their opinions of your leadership style which can feel very personal.

Increasingly, employers are grappling with this demanding new reality, which requires taking a fresh perspective on leadership and developing a new set of skills. It also requires a new level of self-awareness.

As a leader you're called to be a mentor, teacher, coach, problem solver, advocate, innovator, nurturer, enforcer, and so much more. All while protecting your organization's reputation, driving the company agenda, improving efficiencies and growing profit margins. Tired yet? You're also expected to be a self-sacrificing servant, happy to give all the glory and take all the blame.

These are all important and very real aspects of leadership, but as a human being it's natural to also want to be recognized for your work—for your excellence. When you don't receive the recognition or support you need, you can end up feeling overwhelmed, unappreciated, and exhausted. This is when nagging feelings of disengagement, discontentment, and suffering can set in, and the strain can make you wonder whether you're cut out for leadership at all. The to-do list grows, and emotionally, you don't feel like you can keep up.

So what do you do?

CHOOSING YOUR PATH

I believe most people want to do something meaningful and impactful through their work. I suspect you are no different. The truth is that you could do a million other jobs that would be less stressful, less challenging, and probably pay more per hour. However, when you're called, you're called.

I believe YOU will be a good leader *if* that's what you choose to do!

Or maybe you already are, and you just want some help filling that hole in your soul. I get it—you want to be as fulfilled as you are busy. I've been there. My hope for you is that as you learn from my experience, research, and real-world stories, you will feel encouraged to grow as a person who loves what you do, spreads joy, and brings your gifts to the world through your work in the way that only you can.

Being a leader isn't easy. You'll take on a ton of responsibility and face tremendous pressure to produce results. Sometimes, you'll feel overwhelmed by all the expectations. On the other hand, leadership isn't reserved for the enlightened. You're not expected to know, or be, everything. With all the leadership quotes and platitudes out there, you might have gotten the idea that you should lead like Mahatma Gandhi, or Mother Teresa, or Martin

Luther King, Jr. Nobody should be held to these ridiculous standards of "great leadership." Yes, there's plenty to learn from these luminary leaders, but let's get real. You live in your world. Your leadership skills will be honed through your experiences in that world, and your perspective will be shaped by your particular situation, your team's needs, and who you decide to be as a leader.

As hard as it may be to lead others, it can also be extremely rewarding. The fact that you've picked up this book means you know that, you take it seriously, and you want to do it well. As you move through this guide, I encourage you to commit to being honest with yourself. Self-awareness is not always an easy thing, but if you'll take some time to really consider the questions this book poses and discover what leadership means to you, you'll come out the other side miles ahead of other people, professionally *and* personally. Reading *Leadership—Love It or Leave It* is your opportunity to choose for yourself if leadership is right for you.

THE JOURNEY AHEAD

This book is designed to help you get clear on what it really means to be a leader, why you want to lead, and offer some tools and insights for loving leadership. As you read each chapter, consider where you are on your own journey. Take time to understand why you've made the choice to be a leader—or not—and decide who you want to be. This foundation will help you navigate all the challenges that will come your way.

Along your journey, you will inevitably continue to hear countless opinions from the rest of the world about who you *should* be and what you *should* do. Regardless of the messages you're receiving, the question you need to answer for yourself is: do you really want to lead others? Try to remember: this is your journey.

I want to support you in your leadership journey. In the back of this book, you'll find my email address. If you ever have a thought to share or a question to ask, please don't hesitate to send a message. I *love* connecting with people at every stage of the leadership journey, wherever they happen to be in the world, so go ahead and email me. As long as I'm out here causing trouble, I'll reply and share what I know, and if I can't answer your questions, I'll refer you to someone who can.

I firmly believe that when you understand leadership, value the responsibility, connect your personal "why" to your work, and bring your whole self to it, you will be a fabulous, fulfilled leader that people want to follow—a leader that positively impacts lives, organizations, and ultimately the world.

So, let's get started.

CHAPTER 1

HUMAN SUFFERING... AT WORK

Some people happily eat, sleep, and breathe their jobs, like my friend Michelle, the recruiter who never stops recruiting.

I went to lunch with her recently. We chose a side booth, hoping for some quiet space so we could catch up. Leaning across the table, Michelle was sharing a story with me when she suddenly stopped talking, mid-sentence. Silent, she sat back and tilted her head so her ear was pressed against the booth behind her.

"Everything all right?" I asked.

"Shhhh," she whispered. "Hang on!"

Then she grabbed something out of her purse, scooted out of her seat, flipped around and introduced herself to the couple having lunch behind her. After a few minutes, she returned to her seat.

"Someone you know?" I asked.

"No," she said. "I thought I heard them say something about their son finishing his residency at the medical center, and I wanted to see if he was a family medicine doctor. We're looking for a couple to add to our team. I gave them my card, but I got his name and I know where he is working, so I'll be calling him tonight!"

With a gleam in her eye, she jotted down some notes on the back of a receipt, and we picked up right where we left off.

This kind of thing happens all the time with Michelle. She's a recruiter for a healthcare system, but ask her what she does and she'll tell you, "I help other people find a job they'll love as much as I love mine." And she means it. She whole-heartedly believes in her organization and is personally committed to what they work to accomplish. She invests personal time and emotional energy with her recruits, getting to know them, their families, and their professional goals to ensure a good fit. Losing a candidate is painful for her, and successfully recruiting good candidates to the organization is fulfilling; their success feels like her success. She is committed to producing the best outcomes for everyone involved.

Impromptu restaurant conversations aren't part of her job description, but she'll do it every time. Because for Michelle, it's personal.

Michelle has the ideal work situation; the kind we would all like to have. She doesn't struggle with finding work-life balance because her career is an integrated part of her life. She views her work as an extension of who she is and what she wants to do. Michelle is the living embodiment of "do what you love, and you'll never work a day in your life."

ENGAGEMENT

Michelle is the kind of employee every company wants—they'd love to have a long roster of Michelles on their team. That's because, as a wholly invested employee, Michelle represents the holy grail of corporate success—employee engagement.

What is employee engagement? Here is a very brief and incomplete history:

Long before the pursuit of employee engagement, researchers, businesses, and even the military have been interested in understanding what motivates and drives the performance of human beings at work. Leaders and business owners have especially had a vested interest in figuring out the secret formula for increasing human production and commitment to work. And that pursuit has gone through many iterations and names through the decades.

After the Industrial Revolution, work became highly standardized with a focus on mass production, efficiency, and increased throughput of employees on the "line." The goals of factory and business owners in the late nineteenth century were clear—get more production out of employees while reducing costs. Motivation during this time was more about the stick than the carrot. Do what you're told for as long as you're told or else.

"Stick" motivation followed the American worker into the twentieth century with Frederick Taylor's theory of scientific management. Under this theory, workers in the early 1900s were subject to efforts to make them more efficient—think stopwatches and motion studies—while the "brain work" of management was clearly delineated from the "task work" done on the factory floor. Taylor's theory was, as you might imagine, highly controversial, but is also credited for establishing many foundational management principles that modern-day management was built upon.

It turned out, of course, that all employees, and the work they did, benefited from a more human approach to management. In the 1920s, a series of studies known as The Hawthorne Experiments began to make this clear. Conducted over nine years by Elton Mayo, a professor of Industrial Management at Harvard Business School and his protégé Fritz Roethlisberger at Western Electric, these studies began with a goal of determining the effects of lighting, work hours, breaks, and physical environment on worker productivity.[1] However, the researchers also discovered that the very act of observing and interviewing workers seemed to cause changes in worker behavior.

In what may have been the first recorded employee feedback sessions, Mayo and Roethlisberger directed a series of interviews with employees who were able to speak freely about whatever they wanted to discuss. When their comments were compiled and used to set policy and address working conditions, productivity rose. The Hawthorne Studies concluded that when employers take an interest in workers and make decisions based on their natural needs and psychological makeup, productivity increases.[2] Imagine that! While there is still academic debate around the methodology and interpretation of the

---

[1] Mihel Anteby and Rakesh Khurana, "A New Vision: An Essay," *Harvard Business School Baker Library Historical Collection,* https://www.library.hbs.edu/hc/hawthorne/anewvision.html.

[2] "What is the Human Relations Movement?" *HRZone,* https://www.hrzone.com/hr-glossary/what-is-the-human-relations-movement.

studies', the Hawthorne Studies are important because they introduced the human relations movement—a focus on the employee's social and psychological needs to drive performance.

Over the next few decades, numerous ideas and theories on employee morale, job satisfaction, work design, culture, and employee commitment would find their way into management journals, consulting circles, and boardrooms.

The term "engagement" was first introduced in a 1990 *Academy of Management Journal* by pioneering researcher Dr. William Kahn, a professor of Organizational Behavior at Boston University's Questrom School of Business. Dr. Kahn is recognized as the founding father of engagement.[3] As Kahn says:

> The engagement idea offers a way to think more deeply about the choices that individuals make, consciously and not, about how much of their personal selves they wish to bring in and express in the conduct of their work roles.[4]

For Dr. Kahn, engagement with work was personal. It was

---

[3] William A. Kahn, "Psychological Conditions of Personal Engagement and Disengagement at Work," *Academy of Management Journal*, 33, no. 4 (December 1990): 692-724.

[4] David Zinger, "William Kahn: Q&A With the Founding Father of Engagement (Part 1)," *TalentSpace Blog*, January 23, 2017, http://publicaffairs-sme.com/PatriotFamily/wp-content/uploads/2015/01/Personal-engagement-not-employee-engagement.pdf.

a decision based on what he calls personal presence—comprised of physical, cognitive, and emotional presence.

While he is credited with establishing the concept of employee engagement, organizations have strayed from Dr. Kahn's foundational focus on the individual and how he or she chooses to show up and interact with others and the work itself. Dr. Kahn was dismayed by the shift in focus from personal to employee engagement. When asked about it in an interview, Dr. Kahn had this to say:

> I very deliberately focused on "personal" engagement—the harnessing of the person in the context of role performances. This refers to the thoughts, feelings, and energies of who people are when they are at their best selves. The focus, frankly, is on whether people can express their selves in the context of their work roles, which enables them to grow and evolve even as they are performing well.
>
> The shift in the industry to 'employee' engagement is, in many ways, a reversal of that idea, and of my intention. The industry focus is on how leaders can get people to work harder and with more energy on behalf of their organizations, with less focus on whether people are bringing their best, cherished selves into that work. I think that the power of the ideas about personal engagement gets lost in that reimagined focus.[5]

---
5 Zinger, "William Kahn."

Whatever Dr. Kahn's intention, once the engagement concept was out of the bag, it very quickly took on a life of its own. By the time we entered the twenty-first century, most of the major business consulting firms had begun offering their own unique theories, definitions, and programs promising to drive employee engagement.

One of the bigger players in the game was Gallup, a polling company turned research and management consulting company. In the mid-1990s, Gallup developed a twelve-question survey called Q12 to measure employee engagement for businesses. Every day, for many years, the Q12 poll tracked people nationally and publicly reported employee engagement rates. They continue to track and report engagement statistics on a monthly basis today, making them one of the most quoted sources on employee engagement in the country.

Today, there are countless additional surveys, studies, and research testifying to the benefits of employee engagement for the company, including increased productivity, higher customer satisfaction, profitability, retention, quality, and decreased safety incidents, absenteeism, and turnover. If those incentives aren't compelling enough, studies also indicate that businesses with the highest levels of employee engagement are likely to outperform their competitors in categories such as share growth, customer engagement, productivity, retention, safety, and profitability.[6]

EMPLOYEE ENGAGEMENT DEFINED

Clearly, employee engagement is good for business. Organizations are eager to reap the rewards of "high employee engagement." But what, exactly, is it?

If you Google "employee engagement definition" you'll get about 85 million results in .4 seconds. A quick review of the search results makes it seem like there may be 85 million different definitions, but there are a few common threads. See if you can find them in these definitions:

- "An 'engaged employee' is defined as one who is fully absorbed by and enthusiastic about their work and so takes positive action to further the organization's reputation and interests."[7]
- "Employee engagement is the extent to which employees feel passionate about their jobs, are committed to the organization, and put discretionary effort into their work."[8]

---

[6] Jim Harter, "Employee Engagement on the Rise in the U.S.," *Gallup News*, August 26, 2018, https://news.gallup.com/poll/241649/employee-engagement-rise.aspx

[7] "Employee Engagement," *Wikipedia*, last edited March 19, 2019, https://en.wikipedia.org/wiki/Employee_engagement.

[8] "What is Employee Engagement?" *Custom Insight*, https://www.custominsight.com/employee-engagement-survey/what-is-employee-engagement.asp.

- "Employee engagement is the emotional attachment employees feel toward their place of work, job role, position within the company, colleagues, and culture and the affect this attachment has on well-being and productivity."[9]
- "The term *employee engagement* relates to the level of an employee's commitment and connection to an organization."[10]
- "Gallup defines engaged employees as those who are involved in, enthusiastic about, and committed to their work and workplace."[11]

Did you notice how many of the words used in these definitions refer to feelings? Words like passion, commitment, emotional attachment, connection, and enthusiastic. Many articles and definitions also refer to the amount of discretionary effort (effort beyond what is required or expected) the employee provides the organization because of all those feelings.

So engagement is a feeling? Yes. Yes, it is. And, as we've seen, for businesses it can be a very lucrative feeling.

---

9 "What is Employee Engagement?" *HRZone*, https://www.hrzone.com/hr-glossary/what-is-employee-engagement.

10 "Developing and Sustaining Employee Engagement," *SHRM*, https://www.shrm.org/resourcesandtools/tools-and-samples/toolkits/pages/sustainingemployeeengagement.aspx.

11 "U.S. Employee Engagement," *Gallup Daily*, https://news.gallup.com/poll/180404/gallup-daily-employee-engagement.aspx.

The thing is, Dr. Kahn was right—engagement is a personal choice. I've seen it time and time again over the course of twenty years in human resources—you can't *make* someone feel committed or emotionally attached. (Or, if you can, it's no easy task. I'd probably still be married if it were.) But that's exactly what companies are trying to do. Businesses spend hundreds of millions of dollars every year on surveys, strategies, and solutions to make employees feel more committed to what they do, where they do it, and who they do it with. Money spent to make employees *want* to give more of their time, creativity, and energy. More of themselves. And this is what makes engagement such a slippery slope.

Work at its core is simply an exchange. An exchange of time and talent to produce specific outcomes for compensation at a rate agreed upon by both the employee and the employer. Yet, when employers pursue employee engagement for all the wonderful benefits it may yield, they're upping the ante. And while employee engagement has a softer feel and ideally genuine concern for the person, the goal seems a little reminiscent of the ideals that came before it—figure out how to get more than has originally been agreed upon, willingly, if not enthusiastically, from the employee.

The reality is that companies can't buy or strategize the type of engagement that someone like Michelle brings to her work. While her organization can provide an environment that supports Michelle in doing work that she finds meaningful; only she can decide to bring her enthusiasm, commitment, emotional attachment, and the one hundred ten percent to her work that the company craves. Engagement is personal. *Your* meaning, your enthusiasm, your commitment, your emotional attachment, and your extra 10 percent are your decision. *Your* engagement is personal.

As compelling as employee engagement is for the company, and even for you and I to be doing work that we feel so committed to—most of us aren't feeling it.

DISENGAGEMENT HURTS MORE THAN THE BOTTOM LINE

Case in point: Susan.

Susan is a coaching client of mine from New York. She was a trained accountant working for a public accounting firm when we started working together. I'll never forget a conversation we had early in our partnership:

"Hey Susan, how are you?"

"I'm good. Well, pretty good. I almost got in a wreck today."

"Oh my gosh are you ok?" I asked.

"Oh, yeah, we didn't actually hit. The car in front of me slammed on their brakes, and I was sure the guy behind me was going to plow into the back of my car. But he stopped in time."

"Well that's good, but that must have been a scary way to start the day. "

"Well actually, I was kind of disappointed that he didn't hit me."

"What?"

"I know…that's crazy, right?"

I laughed. "Crazy is relative around here. Tell me more."

"Well, I found myself thinking if I had a minor accident, I might be able to skip at least half the day of work to take care of it. I can't believe I'm even saying that. I would rather get in a car wreck than go to work. What is wrong with me?"

"I'm pretty sure there's nothing *wrong* with you. Tell me what makes a car wreck sound better than a day at work."

"I don't know exactly. I used to love accounting—like, I'm a complete nerd for numbers and spreadsheets. But I feel like I sort of hate it right now."

I pressed for more. "Is it the accounting work that you don't enjoy anymore?"

"No. I don't know. Maybe it's this place. I feel like I just don't belong here. It sucks the life out of me. And for what? A boss that expects entirely too much, people I don't connect with, and ridiculous hours. I feel like I never see my two boys awake during the week and I'm completely exhausted by the time the weekend rolls around. I don't have the energy to play with my kids or hang out with my husband, much less look for another job. I feel like I'm showing up everywhere but not really being present anywhere."

Sound familiar?

Unfortunately, it probably does. Gallup reports that over the last eighteen years of tracking, only about 30 percent of the U.S. workforce, on average, have been engaged at work and roughly 70 percent of us have not![12] Of that 70 percent, 53 percent have been defined as "not engaged"—they're just there—and around 17 percent as "actively

---

[12] Harter, "Employee Engagement," https://news.gallup.com/poll/241649/employee-engagement-rise.aspx.

disengaged"—they're miserable and, reportedly, destroy all the good stuff engaged employees do.

Maybe organizations would be better served working to determine why we have so much disengagement instead of focusing so much energy on getting more engagement.

EMPLOYEE DISENGAGEMENT DEFINED

You might think so. But when you Google "employee disengagement" you get a measly 795 thousand hits compared to the 85 *million* you get when searching employee engagement.

There is some information there, however. Scroll through a page or two and you'll see lots of articles about how to identify the top signs of disengagement and how to address it, solve it, or otherwise eliminate it. You'll also see a myriad of articles explaining the causes, along with attention-grabbing headlines reporting the enormous costs of employee disengagement to companies. Keep digging and you'll find one of the most commonly cited reports by Gallup, showing that actively disengaged employees cost the U.S. $483 billion to $605 billion each year in lost productivity, creating "an employee engagement crisis, with serious and potentially lasting repercussions for the global economy."[13]

---

13 Annamarie Mann and Jim Harter, "The Worldwide Employee Engagement Crisis," *Gallup Workplace*, January 7, 2016, https://www.gallup.com/workplace/236495/worldwide-employee-engagement-crisis.aspx.

Surprise, surprise—employee disengagement is bad for business. Really bad! Researching definitions makes that crystal-clear. So, what is disengagement?

Defining disengagement is actually much easier than defining its more desirable counter. See if you can pick up the common themes:

- "You don't see [disengaged employees] volunteering for projects or going the extra mile. Their creativity, their ideas, and their suggestions go missing. They show up and they do the bare minimum. They are compliant to stay employed and to not get put on a performance plan."[14]
- "Those who are not engaged…are less likely to put in discretionary effort…emotionally disconnected from their work and workplace and jeopardize their teams' performance."[15]
- "A disengaged employee is someone who usually doesn't enjoy their work…does the bare minimum, doesn't put in extra effort, and is highly unlikely to be a company evangelist…those who are actively dis-

---

14 Todd Davis, "How to Reengage Employees," *FranklinCovery*, May 2017, https://www.franklincovey.com/blog/2017/5/22/how_to_reengage_empl.html.

15 "What is Gallup's Employee Engagement Index and What Does it Measure?" *Gallup*, https://q12.gallup.com/help/en-us/Answers/180023.

engaged are consciously causing problems at their companies."[16]
- *"Disengaged workers*...view their jobs as an exchange of time for a paycheck. They arrive and leave on time, take their breaks, never volunteer for extra work or projects, and do little else in between beyond the minimal effort. They show little passion or creativity for their jobs and go through the motions."[17]
- "Employee disengagement is catastrophic to any organization since it results in low employee productivity. Disengaged employees only do what is required of them sometimes amid complaints, they avoid doing extra, they tend to take more sick days and exhibit low morale."
- "Disengaged employees are not poised to put in extra effort for success. They don't like going to work most days. They're unlikely to recommend the products of, or employment with, their employer. Laziness, apathy, and dissidence are merely symptoms of bigger problems that can affect employee performance."[18]

So, disengaged employees are emotionally disconnected,

---

[16] Courtney Hart, "What is a Disengaged Employee? How Can You Identify Them?" *Xactly Blog*, February 26, 2015, https://www.xactlycorp.com/blog/spot-disengaged-employee/.

[17] UNC Executive Development, "Engaged, Disengaged, Actively Disengaged. What's the Difference?" *UNC Executive Development Blog*, March 17, 2016, http://execdev.kenan-flagler.unc.edu/blog/engaged-disengaged-actively-disengaged.-whats-the-difference.

[18] David Mizne, "5 Surprising Signs of a Disengaged Employee (Infographic)" *15Five*, https://www.15five.com/blog/5-surprising-signs-of-disengaged-employee/.

unlikely to volunteer, unwilling to put in discretionary effort, or go the extra mile. They're compliant, doing only the bare minimum, and unwilling to promote the business. (Read: no personal feels, no enthusiasm, and no activity beyond the agreed upon exchange.) These are some of the kinder descriptors.

Then there's this one from the most cited source on all things engagement.

- "Of the 70 percent of American workers who are not reaching their full potential, 52 percent are not engaged, and another 18 percent are actively disengaged. These employees are emotionally disconnected from their companies, and may actually be working against their employers' interests; they are less productive, are more likely to steal from their companies, negatively influence their coworkers, miss workdays, and drive customers away."[19]

Gallup characterizes unengaged or actively disengaged employees as not only failing to reach *their* full potential, but also likely to be aggressively undermining their employers. They are even more likely to *steal* from their employers. This troubling representation of a disen-

---

19 Susan Sorenson and Keri Garman, "How to Tackle U.S. Employees' Stagnating Engagement," *Gallup Business Journal*, June 11, 2013, https://news.gallup.com/businessjournal/162953/tackle-employees-stagnating-engagement.aspx.

gaged employee, unfortunately, vilifies the disengaged employee to create a sense of urgency for employers. (You may not be surprised to learn that Gallup sells "the" solution to disengagement.)

In reality, I have rarely encountered an employee working to aggressively undermine their employer or actively take advantage of them. There's a big difference between a bad hire and an emotionally disconnected employee; bad hires are typically easy to identify, counsel, and separate from the organization. Disengaged employees are different. Although businesses may see them as merely the opposite of engaged employees—an enormous cost, a threat to business, or numbers to be converted from one category to another—emotionally disconnected employees are actually suffering human beings.

Disengagement is intensely personal. The disengaged employees I've talked to complain of anxiousness, trouble concentrating, low energy, feeling depressed, being uninterested in and apathetic about work, and not enjoying the things they used to enjoy. They tell me they aren't sleeping, feel irritable, and suffer from headaches and other health problems that just won't go away. Some turn to food, smoking, drinking, or other unhealthy substances to cope with the stress.

My client, Susan, was in no way trying to undermine

the company she worked for nor bring down any of her colleagues. She was getting her work done and meeting expectations, but she was definitely not contributing much discretionary effort or volunteering for extra work. She was compliant but not creative, which was completely unlike her performance with other organizations. Susan was earning her paycheck but suffering personally. She was suffering from fatigue, she felt irritable and withdrawn. Daydreaming about a minor accident to avoid work can never be a healthy sign.

I haven't been exactly where Susan was, but it was close. I experienced heart palpitations, unhealthy weight loss, and muscle pain that my doctors could only attribute to stress. I found myself struggling with uncharacteristic self-doubt and wondering if I was just going crazy. I also felt frustrated—almost angry—more often than I didn't. I didn't know exactly what was happening to me, so I blamed it on everything from stupid people making stupid decisions to ridiculous policy changes and the full moon if that's all I had.

And like Susan, I was extremely withdrawn. I was confused and embarrassed and didn't want anyone to know I was struggling. I was a leader with a lot of responsibilities for heaven's sake. I couldn't tell anyone I felt like I was completely losing my shit. Everyone else seemed fine with the same pressures; I thought I should be able to figure out how to be fine too.

Disengagement isn't just bad for business—disengagement is bad for you, bad for your health, and bad for your relationships. Susan was too drained to play with her children, which left her feeling like a bad mom and her kids wondering what was wrong with Mommy. I've heard many stories of strained relationships and concerned family members over the years. I even got a call or two from worried spouses, like Ron's wife. Ron was really struggling with stress and discontentment, and he'd taken up drinking to cope. When the drinking became excessive, his wife reached out asking for help on his behalf.

Suffering at work doesn't stay at work. Why would it? We talk about work-life balance a lot in our culture; as if there are two versions of ourselves to manage, but that's not true. There's only one you. If work-you is suffering, then life-you is suffering as well.

Of course, disengagement isn't a new experience. We've known about disengagement, or something very much like it, for a long time—we often call it "burnout." Burnout, according to the Mayo Clinic, is a state of physical or emotional exhaustion that also involves a sense of reduced accomplishment and loss of personal identity.[20] It can be caused by excessive workplace stress, pressure to meet constantly increasing expectations and to perform at optimum levels—all the time. Job burnout can result in depression-like symptoms, cynicism, detachment, anxiety, difficulty sleeping and generalized health issues.[21] Sound familiar?

Coincidentally, Gallup has also reported that "organizations are facing an employee burnout crisis." Another crisis? It seems so. (But don't worry—they sell the solution for that crisis as well.)

Which raises the question: in our pursuit of greater engagement, are we actually creating the disengagement we so desperately want to eliminate? Gallup says no, claiming that the burnout crisis is not because of the engagement crisis but in addition to it. According to Gallup, "Burnout [has] less to do with expectations for hard work and high performance—and more to do with how someone is managed."[22] I'm not sure I'm buying it.

---

20 Mayo Clinic, "Job Burnout: How to Spot it and Take Action," *Mayo Clinic Healthy Lifestyle*, November 21, 2018, https://news.gallup.com/businessjournal/162953/tackle-employees-stagnating-engagement.aspx.

21 "Signs of Burnout," *ada*, https://ada.com/signs-of-burnout/.

22 Ben Wigert and Sangeeta Agrawal, "Employee Burnout, Part 1: The 5 Main Causes," *Gallup Workplace*, July 12, 2018, https://www.gallup.com/workplace/237059/employee-burnout-part-main-causes.aspx.

Why *are* so many people suffering in the workplace? Are the majority of people in the workforce generally unhappy people? Are seven out of ten hires bad hires? Is the recruitment process that broken? Is it a culture issue? Is it propaganda for companies in the business of selling productivity, efficiency, and profit?

It may be a "chicken-or-the-egg" dilemma, but what's most important is that you understand the bigger picture—beyond the headlines. Whatever we call it—employee disengagement, burnout, or the next trending term—the suffering is real. It may not be the "crisis" we're being sold, but where it does exist, it isn't simply a ding to the bottom line. It is deeply impactful to the human being experiencing it.

UNDERSTANDING THE "WHY"

Every author (winking right at you), expert, and consulting group has a different opinion on what drives engagement and disengagement, but they do agree on one big "why": leaders. Leaders have tremendous influence over how smoothly or how stressful work goes for their employees and coworkers.

You may not be surprised to learn that most of us have left at least one job just to get away from a bad manager. I know I have. In fact, studies and surveys suggest that

50 to 70 percent of working adults have done this. One employee engagement study determined that "Poor relationships between employees and their managers are a leading cause, if not the leading cause, of employee disengagement." The study looked at eighteen thousand employees across more than one hundred and fifty organizations, and instead of focusing solely on what drove engagement, the researchers analyzed the drivers of disengagement. Guess what they found? When they studied the bottom 10 percent, or the most disengaged, they found that five of the top ten drivers were directly related to the employee's experience with their immediate manager. That finding was supported by our friends at Gallup who reported that "managers account for at least 70 percent variance in employee engagement scores."[23] Willis Towers Watson also reported that "employees with effective senior leaders and managers are much more likely to be highly engaged."[24]

Leaders have the most direct influence on an employee's ability and willingness to personally connect with their work and their organization. As we've seen, that connection has an impact on their productivity, well-being, and

---

23 Randall Beck and Jim Harter, "Managers Account for 79% of Variance in Employee Engagement," *Gallup Business Journal*, April 21, 2015, https://news.gallup.com/businessjournal/182792/managers-account-variance-employee-engagement.aspx.

24 WillisTowersWatson, "Reset Leadership Expectations to Engage Today's Workforce," *WillisTowersWatson Perspectives*, 2017, https://www.willistowerswatson.com/-/media/WTW/PDF/Insights/2017/06/reset-leadership-expectations-to-engage-today-workforce.

overall engagement. This means that leaders not only have the ability to support engagement, they also have the ability to create disengagement.

So, the majority of the workforce is considered disengaged; they're suffering, and leaders are to blame. That's a lot of responsibility to put on leaders, especially when you consider that managers, the very people with the most potential impact on employee engagement, are just about as disengaged as everybody else. It turns out that only 35 percent of managers are engaged, which means 65 percent of them are suffering the challenges and symptoms of disengagement too. That's only slightly less than the 70 percent of non-management employees.

In reality, the disengagement rate for leaders is probably higher. As you move up the hierarchy of management, the pool of people participating in engagement surveys gets much smaller. Managers may be reluctant to respond honestly if they think they'll be identified as the "squeaky wheel" that's bringing the organization's engagement "score" down. If company culture doesn't support transparency, they may perceive an honest response to be a potentially career-limiting move.

For example, let me share the story of one organization I worked with. This organization went through a tremendous amount of operational and leadership change very quickly. Practically everything employees understood about the organization had changed in less than a year. A series of bumbled communications, payroll errors, and failed IT integrations created an atmosphere of confusion and left employees feeling deceived, left out of decisions that impacted them, and abandoned by top-level leadership. As a result, the organization experienced a 60 percent drop in their employee engagement ranking. No surprise there.

The big shock? The leadership engagement rankings. They didn't budge! Engagement rates for leadership remained the same as the prior year. Were the leaders in between front line and senior-level staff less impacted or somehow insulated from all of the changes happening? No! The leaders were no more engaged and no less exhausted and worried about their futures than their teams. They just didn't dare to say so. Even though the company said they wanted honest feedback, the actual culture did not support that level of honest dialogue. The leaders didn't feel safe sharing their truth. They experienced the same apathy and disconnectedness as their employees. The truth was, the leaders who had the most direct influence on non-management employees were suffering too.

If disengagement creates suffering at the employee level, how much more damaging is disengagement at the leadership level?

Here's the thing—nothing magical happens to you when you step into a leadership role. Fears and anxieties don't simply disappear. You are still an employee facing the same challenges of making your own emotional connection with work. The only difference is that now you have the added challenges of motivating and influencing others. As a leader you have the ability—the responsibility—to have a positive impact on the human beings looking to you for support, guidance, and vision.

How do you *learn* to do that? Most organizations and leadership "training" programs do a terrible job of informing and preparing you to step into that responsibility. To end the real suffering that happens at work (disengagement), we have to get real and get personal about what leadership really is, why you want it, and how leadership serves you. We have to ask these questions *before* asking you to serve others in the context of work. To break the cycle of disengagement, we must start with our leaders.

Let me be clear here; I'm not anti-organization; I'm just seriously pro-you.

Leadership is hard and it is not for everyone. We don't like to talk about it, but it's true. You're contending with wily human beings who bring their own ideas, motivations, and issues to work each day. Organizations today demand more for less and it's your responsibility to meet those demands, even in a constantly changing environment. If you're set up with unrealistic expectations, vague definitions, and bullshit platitudes about "great" leadership, you'll be overwhelmed no matter how professionally accomplished you are.

Don't get me wrong. Because leadership is challenging, all leaders struggle. If you are or decide to become a leader, you will too. That doesn't mean you shouldn't be one. If you can approach the decision to lead and the inherent challenges with intention, self-awareness, and learning, you may be able to alleviate suffering for yourself and those counting on you.

Yes, leadership is hard. Really hard. But it can also be one of the most rewarding roles if it's the right one for you.

YOU FIRST

The goal for this book is not to solve the "engagement crisis," or whatever "crisis" comes next. I want to help you decide if leadership is right *for you*. Leaders have tremendous impact and responsibility. To make a positive impact, you've got to love this leadership thing. You have to find joy in leading other people, or you're going to suffer and cause suffering for those around you, even if unintentionally. And there's way too much of that going on!

Successful and fulfilling leadership starts and ends with you. We can't begin to talk about you being a "successful" leader until we talk about whether or not you even *want to be* a leader. Too often, people accept leadership roles without any thoughtful consideration beyond the money, status, or perks of the job. The disengagement rates prove that there is more to consider. You need to understand what it means to be a leader today, get clear about why you want to do it, and define who you want to be as a leader. *Then* we can talk about what successful, loving leadership looks like in action.

TOUGH-LOVE QUESTIONS

Tough-Love Questions throughout the book are meant to challenge and inspire you at any stage of your leadership journey.

NEW OR ASPIRING LEADER

In this chapter, you've learned that engagement is defined as an employee's personal commitment or obligation to their work or their organization.

- What does it mean for YOU to really be engaged in your own work?
- Think of a time when you found yourself emotionally involved and personally committed to what you were

doing. What feelings did you experience? How was your performance?
- Now think of a time when you found yourself not really connected emotionally or personally to what you were doing. What feelings did you experience? How was your performance?

EXPERIENCED LEADER

You've been in a leadership role for a while, and you've probably seen engaged and disengaged employees. Even if your organization doesn't conduct formal surveys, you've seen the difference engagement can make in the workplace. Take a moment and do a pulse check on your own engagement. Answer honestly—there's no one here but me and you.

- How emotionally involved or personally committed do you feel to your work right now?
- Whom did you most identify with in this chapter? Michelle or Susan?

A PERSONAL NOTE ABOUT ENGAGEMENT

If you are sensing a bit of attitude from me on the topic of measuring engagement, it is for good reason. The more I have researched the topic, the more frustrated and concerned I have become.

I've had ample opportunity to experience the good, the bad, and the flat out ridiculousness in the arena of employee engagement. I've had the good fortune to work with some senior leadership teams that truly wanted to figure out how to improve the emotional well-being and job satisfaction of their employees. And I've also worked for the other guys.

Employee engagement is a "score" for the other guys to increase by a certain margin to reach their annual bonus goals. I've even worked for the guys who added the employee engagement score to the list of goals for the employee incentive program. Yes, you read that right. If the employees reported that they were engaged and satisfied then it helped them meet their own bonus goals. Anyone see the conflict here?

Employee engagement, for some, has morphed into a very organization-centric, score-based pursuit predicated on all of the studies indicating more engagement equals more profit.

Disengagement is all too often propagated as "crisis" by organizations that sell a "solution." Packaged best practices promise to improve margins, raise employee productivity, and increase retention. But if you consider that these solutions have been tried for over fifteen years with little to no improvement in "engagement," you'll see that they haven't solved "the engagement crisis." It doesn't make sense.

Let me be clear, I'm not throwing shade on corporate leaders for implementing engagement programs. The pursuit of engagement as a means to improve job satisfaction, employee relations, or employee well-being and self-actualization in the workplace is admirable. Businesses that have an "engaged" workforce experience tremendous benefits, as do many individuals. I would, however, encourage our corporate leaders to consider what exactly they are really after in their pursuit of engagement. Is it the benefits your organization stands to gain? Is it the genuine belief that your people are the most important aspect of your business? Or is it both?

To find out, you have to define what employee engagement means for *your* organization and get clear on *why* you're hopping on the engagement train *before* you invest in and initiate programs to engage your employees. Chasing employee engagement for the sake of improved business performance isn't wrong, but representing it as anything more is a misleading strategy that may actually do more harm than good to your business and your people. I encourage you to tackle employee engagement with the same level of research, clarity, and transparency you would approach any other business decision. You'll stand a better chance of getting the results you're after.

CHAPTER 2

THIS AIN'T YOUR GRANDPA'S LEADERSHIP

Ms. Noel, I'm sending you this email to let you know that your daughter will be receiving an award at next Friday's Celebration of Learning ceremony held in the school auditorium. Brennan is such an exceptional student and I love having her in my class.—Ms. Donohue

I sat up a little taller in my chair and a smile made its way across my face as I read the message from my daughter's kindergarten teacher. B's getting an award! That's so cool! I read on.

"I hope that you'll be able to attend to see Brennan get this quarter's Leadership Award!"

A what?!? She's getting a *leadership* award? That can't be right. There has to be a mistake—a typo maybe. I knew my daughter was smart, attentive, and maybe even a little advanced as a student, but a leader? Back then my daughter was a bit shy and preferred blending in over standing out in almost every situation. But maybe kindergarten was bringing her out of her shell. Curious, I emailed a reply.

> Ms. Donohue, thanks for letting me know. I'll definitely be there. I'm really proud that Brennan is doing so well in your class. Can you tell me what leadership behaviors she has demonstrated to earn the Leadership Award? I'd love to nurture those things at home too. Thank you.—Angie

Her reply:

> That's great. Yes. Brennan is always the first in line, she does what she's asked to do without any fussing, she follows the rules, and sets a really good example for the other students. She really is so sweet and such a joy to have in class. See you next Friday.—Ms. D

Well that explains it, I thought. My daughter was extremely compliant back then. More like deathly afraid of breaking a rule. (Not sure if that came from six years of daycare or being the daughter of an HR leader? I'm not proud of either.)

I'm sure Ms. D was thrilled to have a compliant, example-setting rule follower in a classroom of twelve six-year-olds. I would be too, but what was that award teaching my daughter about leadership? Maybe in kindergarten compliance is leadership, but that doesn't match any of the definitions I've ever seen.

DEFINITIONS OF LEADERSHIP

What is leadership, then?

After reading hundreds of books and quotes on leadership trying to define what it actually is, I still didn't know. So I Googled "leadership." Surely Google has the definition. I got 2.9 billion results. There are as many definitions of leadership as there are people trying to define it. Here are a few that stand out:

"My definition of a leader is a man who can persuade people to do what they don't want to do, or do what they're too lazy to do, and like it."

HARRY S. TRUMAN

"A leader is a dealer in hope."

NAPOLEON BONAPARTE

"Leadership is the art of mobilizing others to want to struggle for shared aspirations."

JAMES KOUZES AND BARRY POSNER

"A leader has to be somebody who's getting people to do things which don't seem to make sense to them or are not in their best interests by convincing people that they should work 14 hours a day so that someone else can make more money."

SCOTT ADAMS, CREATOR OF *DILBERT*

"He who cannot be a good follower cannot be a good leader."

ARISTOTLE

"A genuine leader is not a searcher for consensus, but a molder of consensus."

MARTIN LUTHER KING, JR.

"I suppose leadership at one time meant muscles, but today it means getting along with people."

MAHATMA GANDHI

"Leadership is innovation."

STEVE JOBS

Well, that clears it up.

LEADERSHIP IS SITUATIONAL

If you are still unsure what exactly leadership is, you're not alone. It's difficult to define, because real leadership is contextual and circumstantial. Different situations, circumstances, and environments call for different skills, qualities, and styles.

Not long ago I accompanied Daniel, a coaching client, to an event where he presented a keynote speech to hundreds of recent college graduates. Many of the students found him after the event to ask him for pointers on getting "a leadership job." On our flight back we talked about how those new grads perceived leadership as a job title. Daniel insisted that they were right—"no title, no authority, no leadership," he said.

I disagreed. I asked Daniel who the leader on this flight was.

Without hesitation Daniel replied, "It's the pilot, of course, that's why they call him the Captain."

"What about the flight attendant?" I asked.

"Nope," he said. "They're more like hostesses in the sky, here for your comfort and safety."

I persisted. "What if the plane starts going down, and

the pilot is busy trying to get it back in the air? Who's the leader then?"

Daniel smirked.

I said, "I don't know about you, but if something goes wrong on this flight, I'm going to listen to every word that flight attendant says so I know what's going on and just exactly how much freaking out I should be doing. I'm going to happily do exactly what she says to do until we reach the ground, which I presume is a shared goal. In that situation, that 'hostess' will get my undivided attention, and she will influence and guide my actions in pursuit of a common goal."

"Isn't that leadership?"

"Yes," Daniel admitted, "but that's in *that* situation."

Exactly. It works the same way in business. Different stages in your company's growth will require different skill sets, personalities, and leadership styles to support and influence the outcomes you seek.

THE IMPORTANCE OF A GOOD FIT

One size does not fit all.

Once, I worked with a hospital that had experienced a lot

of turnover on one particularly "high-spirited" surgical unit. The nursing staff on the unit was very experienced and very vocal about damn near everything—good or bad. Shannon, the manager of the unit, was really struggling. She was extremely friendly, approachable, and accommodating. Too accommodating. Most of the staff had initially been happy with Shannon, but that was no longer true. Trying to keep everyone happy, Shannon had made special staffing deals and arrangements with several of the nurses, which pissed off everyone else. So she tried to accommodate them too and couldn't. Soon, she faced many unfilled shifts and unhappy people. By the time I got involved, there was a full-blown mutiny going on. With a little coaxing, Shannon agreed that she was in the wrong role and, rather happily, stepped down.

We had been interviewing Meg for another position when all of this went down with Shannon. Meg was former military and had a ton of experience with crisis situations. She was much more rigorous than Shannon and not nearly as warm and fuzzy, but we convinced her to take on the role. At first, there were numerous complaints about Meg's straightforward style and the difficult schedule changes she implemented. Within a few months, however, the team loved her. They appreciated the consistency, structure, and fairness that Meg brought to the unit.

The hospital had initially thought they needed someone like Shannon to smooth things over and give the employees lots of love and attention. That's nice, but it wasn't what the unit needed. It needed someone strong who wouldn't take any crap. Someone to create consistency and structure and help the team get things done efficiently. Someone these experienced and passionate nurses could respect whether they agreed with her or not. Not just a leader, but the right leader with the right skills and personality for the job.

Successful leadership is situational: those nurses, on that unit, in that hospital, at that time, needed Meg. Meg would not have done well in a group that needed a softer touch, but her skills and style were perfect for this situation. And while Shannon struggled on the surgical unit, she was a really effective leader on the pediatric unit where scheduling and personalities were more stable and consistent. Different situations, circumstances, and environments call for different skills, qualities, and styles.

MORE DEFINITIONS OF LEADERSHIP

If there is no single definition of good leadership though, why do so many leadership "experts" seem to have *the* definition—conveniently, the one that matches their model? Because as Barbara Kellerman, author of *The End of Leadership* said, "Teaching how to lead is where the money is."

Companies spend hundreds of thousands of dollars annually training their leaders to be more efficient, effective, and productive. Leadership training is a $50 billion a year industry. It's everywhere. You don't have to look too hard to find experts selling their proven three-step path to successful leadership, or articles that preach the "essential" qualities of great leadership. This "news" always seems to come under headlines such as "5 Must-Haves," or "22 Indispensable Qualities." An article recently posted on LinkedIn was actually titled "100 Leadership Skills You Need to be Successful This Year." 100? Is that all? I think they were looking for Jesus.

All of those definitions and "essential" qualities make it sound like you must have superpowers if you are going to be a good leader. But if you're still waiting for your magic wand, let me remind you, nothing magical happens the moment you're promoted. You are still a human being, only now you are inundated with messages of how virtuous you should be. You'll hear that leaders should sacrifice and expect nothing in return, that they should be generous with praise while accepting responsibility, and that they should seek only to recognize, never to be recognized. It's all about servanthood, self-sacrifice, and service at all costs now, right?

Let's get real. Consider the quotes earlier in this chapter. Do you really aspire to be a dealer of hope? Or did you get into leadership to mobilize others to want to struggle? Should we add "water-walker" and "saver of lost souls" to the list?

With the incredibly high expectations and idealized standards we ask leaders to meet, it's no wonder so many are struggling with disengagement, stress, or overwhelm. I mean, come on, this is work—not martyrdom. The reality of leadership, especially in the twenty-first century, is that you will be called on to be and do many different things—in my own career and role as an HR leader, I was expected to be a coach, counselor, cheerleader, terminator, visionary, firefighter, party planner, disciplinarian, truth teller, secret keeper, and more. Water-walking is usually optional.

In the complex situations most leaders face, a single definition of leadership cannot possibly suffice. As the French poet, novelist, and critic Remy de Gourmont said, "A definition is like a sack of flour compressed into a thimble." Could we ever fit all that leadership inside a single container? Is leadership a role? Is it a position? Is it a list of attributes? Is it the exercise of influence? A process? A set of traits? A form of persuasion? Inducing compliance? A means of motivating? The answer to all of these questions and more is yes. There's just not enough room in one definition to cover all of the facets of leadership.

That said, sometimes simple is best. The simplest definition of leadership is Merriam Webster's: "the power or ability to lead others."

Under this definition, a leader is one who accepts and exercises that power and ability. A leader's effectiveness, in turn, depends on his or her skills, the environment, and the willingness of their followers. Leadership is more than the platitudes we're fed, larger than a single definition, or simply a measure of success. Real leadership is contextual and circumstantial.

THE GLORIFICATION OF LEADERSHIP

Regardless of how it's defined, leadership is the goal for many people in our culture. It has been glamorized to such an extent that we all believe we must aspire to leadership if we hope to be truly successful. For my daughter, it started in kindergarten, and I don't expect it will end there. Leadership is encouraged, recognized, and rewarded throughout the entire school experience. Remember high school? Captain of the football team, head cheerleader, student body president, Spanish club treasurer. All of these coveted roles were rewarded with popularity, recognition, and early leadership experience, which is especially useful in the college admissions process. And if college admissions tell us anything about the societal glorification of leadership, then it's no wonder we take leadership so seriously; here's how college admissions offices show us whom and what we value, according to Susan Cain in the *New York Times*:

"Today we prize leadership skills above all, and nowhere more than in college admissions.

- Harvard: Harvard's application informs students that its mission is 'to educate our students to be citizens and citizen-leaders for society.'[25]
- Yale: Yale's website advises applicants that it seeks 'the leaders of their generation.'
- Princeton: on Princeton's site, 'leadership activities' are first among equals on a list of characteristics for would-be students to showcase."
- Wesleyan: Even a college known for its artistic culture was found by one study to evaluate applicants based on leadership potential. We seem to think that the ideal society is composed of Type A's. It's no longer enough to be a member of the student council; now you have to run the school."

The glorification of leadership extends beyond college. There's a reason we're always talking about "climbing the corporate ladder" and "rising to the top"—most organizations are structured much like the education

---

[25] Susan Cain, "Not Leadership Material? Good. The World Needs Followers (Opinion)," *The New York Times*, March 24, 2017, https://www.nytimes.com/2017/03/24/opinion/sunday/not-leadership-material-good-the-world-needs-followers.html.

experience; they reward management and leadership with titles, perks, and bigger salary ranges. We are quite literally conditioned to believe that the girl at the top is, by definition, winning.

As Barbara Kellerman writes:

> There is also the presumption that being a leader—in sharp contrast to being a follower—is good in and of itself. It is considered a path to having power, authority, influence, and usually, money. And it is considered a path to personal and professional fulfillment as well as to goal achievement, in particular to creating change.

The idea that leadership equals personal and professional success has permeated every industry and practically every area of our lives. But leadership isn't something to mindlessly aspire to, and it isn't the path to success for everyone. It is important, impactful, and always evolving.

LEADERSHIP AND THE NEW WORLD OF WORK

How did we get here?

To get a clearer idea of how leadership has evolved, let's look at some of the historical influences.

After World War II, the traditionalist generation brought

a heavy military influence to the business structure. Titles we use today, like chief executive officer or chief operational officer, came from military nomenclature. Companies also adopted from the military a hierarchical, command-and-control, top-down leadership structure featuring a clear chain of command, hands-on training, and respect for authority. Standardization and strict control of people and processes was the norm, and loyalty to the organization was expected. Leaders of the post–World War II era decided what needed to be done and how employees should do it so that efficiency and productivity were the priority. Command and control leadership was firmly in place.

When the baby boomers came on to the workplace scene, they made some changes, but much remained the same. The boomers introduced new management models that were more collaborative and democratic, but strong hierarchies persisted, and the division between management and staff continued.

Things really began to change when the World Wide Web debuted and access to the internet expanded. As information became more readily available, company leadership could no longer keep authoritarian control over information. There was no more keeping employees in the dark. No more maintaining the status quo, either. Advancements in technology made work faster and more flexible than ever.

Leadership has always been difficult because influencing and managing human beings is, well...hard. But leaders today face unprecedented challenges. Exponential growth and disruptive advancements in technology combined with shifting cultural dynamics and demographics are adding a slew of new leadership "opportunities" to address. One of the greatest opportunities is the generational shift that is playing out across the globe.

A GENERATIONAL SHIFT

For the first time in recorded history, there are four to five generations in the workplace at the same time, and each has a different expectation of how the workplace should operate. In the space below, we will look briefly—and broadly—at the generational attitudes and expectations that currently exist in the workforce. I want to emphasize that none of these descriptions tells the whole story of any generation or any person in that generation, because stereotypes can be dangerous in general, especially in the workplace. Still, we can learn a lot just by looking at the timeline:[26]

- **The traditionalists** (born roughly 1928-45) are in their eighties now, but they're still volunteering and

[26] Michael Dimock, "Defining Generatoins: Where Millennials End and Generation Z Begins," *FactTank*, January 17, 2019, http://www.pewresearch.org/fact-tank/2019/01/17/where-millennials-end-and-generation-z-begins/.

holding fast to the ideals of the command and control hierarchy and a firm commitment to the organization. Many of our foundational leadership ideals were established by this group. A side note: if you have a traditionalist in your life, a grandparent or great-grandparent, I encourage you to talk with them. Get as many stories out of them as you can. This generation had such a massive influence on how this country rose to the economic powerhouse it became.

- **Baby boomers** (born roughly 1946-64) are living longer, staying healthier, and working longer. Many are finding that they must work longer before retiring due to the great recession of 2008, which had a negative impact on retirement savings. A large and competitive generation, Boomers have been dedicated to their work and their organizations for much of their careers. Although tech-savvy, they came before the modern technology shift, and they still value face-to-face communication, personal relationships, and hard work.

- **Generation X** (born roughly 1965-80) is the smallest generation, often referred to as the "middle child" sandwiched between the two larger groups of Boomers and Millennials. Gen Xers came of age with the internet and were mentored professionally by the boomers. This gives the generation a unique blend of digital and traditional leadership styles. They tend to be hyper-collaborative, keep some level of separation

between their work life and personal life, and place a high value on time with family.
- **Generation Y** (born roughly 1981-96), aka the millennial generation, is another massive group in the workforce. As of April 2018 millennials became the largest generation in the workforce, making up 35 percent according to Pew Research.[27] Considered digital natives, this cohort has never existed without technology. The most diverse generation, millennials tend to value flexibility, entrepreneurialism, and purpose in their work. They want work to be a part of their life, more of an experience than a 9 to 5 job, and they are anxious to advance.
- **Gen Z** or post-millennials (born roughly 1997-TBD) are entering college, internships, and entry-level positions now. This group is even more diverse than those that precede it. While it is too early to know how this cohort will behave in the workplace, early indicators point to an "always on" mentality that may impact their expectations of how and where work gets done. Note: the dates that define this generation are still under debate.

Each generation learns and operates in new and different ways, and as these generations work through the

---

[27] Richard Fry, "Millennials Are the Largest Generation in the U.S. Labor Force," *Fact Tank*, April 11, 2018, http://www.pewresearch.org/fact-tank/2018/04/11/millennials-largest-generation-us-labor-force/.

system, organizational culture will shift. But that takes time, something that seems in short supply in this age of accelerated innovation and information transfer.

Advancements occur so rapidly that we've quite literally changed the pace of change. We've moved from typewriters and telephones to tablets and wearables in a relatively short period of time. We now live and work in a world that few could have imagined even thirty years ago. Defining the new world of work in this ever-evolving world is no easy task, but it is exactly what leaders today are helping organizations and the people in them to do.

Leadership is hard and requires a lot of energy, attention, and focus on the well-being of others. As the old adage says, you can't give what you don't have. It all starts with you and your own self-awareness. The next chapter will guide you through understanding why you want to be a leader and help you discover your own motivations and purpose in order to be the best leader you can be, if that's what you choose.

TOUGH-LOVE QUESTIONS
NEW OR ASPIRING LEADER

There are hundreds of definitions of leadership. Answer the following questions to create your own description of the leader you aspire to be.

- How do you define leadership?
- What characteristics, qualities, and behaviors do you associate with good leadership?

EXPERIENCED LEADER

"Good" leadership is often defined by mentors or the organizational culture. Based on your *personal* experience, answer the following questions.

- How do you define leadership for yourself?
- What characteristics, qualities, and behaviors do you associate with good leadership?

THE POWER OF INFLUENCE

What leaders need today, when generational diversity and disruptive advancements are the name of the game, is not a command-and-control attitude. What they need is influence.

Influence is the ability to produce an effect without force or direct exercise of command. It is essentially the ability to produce or impact outcomes through information, motivation, inspiration, and any other indirect means. Influence does not require a title or authority. The ability to influence is one of the most impactful skills any of us, especially leaders, can possess today.

However, influence isn't only impactful for leaders these days. It is also a powerful tool for followers. And leaders require followers.

Today, instead of meeting in the lunchroom or gathering around the water cooler to sound off about a bad boss, an employee can create a whole community on Facebook to weigh in on your management style. Social media gives employees numerous platforms to connect with others and share their satisfaction *and* dissatisfaction.

For example, I worked with a manager who told me that her team didn't like her, and she had no idea why. Maybe she didn't, but everyone else did. It was all over their private Facebook page where they complained that they didn't agree with her philosophy, and they were frustrated and fed up.

The constant urge to connect and share that permeates the social media landscape adds a new layer of responsibility for leaders. Your leadership and what people think of it are reflected on websites that help people decide where they want to work, such as Glassdoor and Indeed. Now more than ever, your employees' thoughts about your behavior and leadership style can directly affect you and your organization's brand.

CHAPTER 3

LEADING ON PURPOSE

Amanda was a passionate, attentive, and caring nurse. She loved her profession. She applied for and got a director level position where she had responsibility for approximately one hundred staff nurses in a newly created unit. The position came complete with a nice pay raise, new office, and impressive title.

After about eight months, however, I was called in to coach Amanda because her senior leaders thought she was struggling. Her staff was complaining, and her metrics were slipping as her goals often went unmet. Amanda couldn't explain why or what she might do about it. She had a lot of "stories" about what was going wrong, but no strategy for fixing things. Amanda had been an exceptional front line supervisor so her senior management was at a loss.

When I met with Amanda, we initially focused on figuring out what was happening with her on a personal level. In the beginning, she was quite short with me and not forthcoming. It didn't take long to recognize that she was totally stressed out.

Over time, she shared her fears and overall struggle. Amanda was absolutely overwhelmed and sleep-deprived from working ten to twelve hours a day. She was also experiencing guilt over missing her kid's baseball and scout activities. Basically, she was a physical and emotional wreck.

In the middle of our coaching, Amanda went on a vacation for a week and a half and completely unplugged from her work and the organization. She came back a new person. She seemed lighter, more confident, and completely present. She was amazed; she hadn't realized how much she was struggling until she took some time away from it all.

Unfortunately, the vacation high didn't last. After a few weeks, Amanda's suffering returned (as did the suffering of her team). She was once again overwhelmed and still didn't have the right answers for her leadership team.

She didn't quit, though. She continued to fight to keep the job that was hurting her, even though she couldn't explain why it was so important to her. She wasn't the primary breadwinner in her family, and she definitely didn't love the work, yet she was suffering and fighting for it.

Ultimately, Amanda was fired. I wasn't surprised; as her coach, I could see Amanda's new position was not a good fit for her skills. After some time, she realized it too. Getting fired turned out to be the best thing that could have happened, because Amanda realized what she really loved—and what she happily returned to—was working closely with her patients.

When we spoke a few months later, she was herself. She was light, smiling, and seemed genuinely happy. She said that she had originally gotten into nursing because she wanted to comfort and heal people. She loved working at the bedside, caring for patients, and seeing real-time outcomes. She had thought that moving up to the next level was what she should do next, but strategic planning, budgeting, and scheduling actually took her away from what she cared about and what she was good at doing.

It's too bad that Amanda figured out her "why" after the fact. If she had been able to truly understand why she wanted the leadership position in the first place, she might never have accepted the new role. The new position didn't match her strengths, what she really loved to do, or why she had gone into nursing. With a little self-awareness, she could have avoided a lot of suffering.

EXPLORING THE "WHY"

Amanda is not alone in jumping into leadership without consciously considering why she wanted to lead. Few of us fully explore the "why."

Even if you ask them why, most people can only explain *how* they became leaders. They'll tell you that they were natural leaders, practically born waiting for someone to direct, something to organize, or some group to influence. Or they might say that they picked "management" as a career path in college and pursued it academically. Some people will share that they were really good at their job and found themselves promoted for their technical expertise to train and lead others doing similar work. Still, others got into leadership because it was the only way to grow in their careers. Notice that a conscious desire to lead doesn't come up a lot in these conversations.

If you fail to carefully consider your personal connection with why you want to lead, it can be easy to rise to a position that you don't really want or aren't suited for. And if the societal assumption is that everyone *should* aspire to leadership, it can be tough to say, "No, thank you" to increased responsibility, including supervisory positions.

I've seen hundreds of performance evaluations that include language like this: "I'd like to see Jane take on more leadership responsibility," or "Jane should work to expand her leadership skills." What if Jane doesn't want to expand her leadership skills? What if Jane is spectacular at what she does because she loves doing it at that level? If, somehow, an employee does manage to pass on a leadership opportunity, it can reflect negatively on future opportunities. This makes gaining clarity on your leadership "why" that much more important.

So why *do* people want to become leaders?

Curious, I conducted a straw poll to learn more. Nearly half of the people I talked with said that being a leader was "just the thing to do," or "the opportunity just presented itself, and I liked it." Money and power were also frequently on the list. The most powerful responses came from people driven by purpose. One was from Lisa, a young professional woman who was in the early stages of her career. Her decision was driven by her faith. "It is my faith. I have a heart for serving others with the highest standards that come from His Word," she said. She had a personal connection to her work and a clear "why." She truly believed that she had a responsibility to lead, teach, and guide others.

One surprising answer came from William, a healthcare

operations executive, whose bad experience with a boss spurred him to enter leadership himself. When he was a young, frontline employee, he'd allegedly made a mistake on the job that could have had harmful results to a patient. It wasn't clear that William was responsible, but the incident shook him badly. When he said as much to his mentor, the only "help" he got was documented corrective action and re-training. After that, William began to doubt his competence, his skills, and his entire career choice. Again, he expressed his feelings and concerns to his mentor, but received very little empathy or coaching on how to manage the emotional aspects of the situation. William almost quit his career before it even got started, but instead, he decided he wanted to make sure things like this didn't happen to other workers. He realized that moving into a leadership role would allow him to support people like himself, so he pursued it.

THE PETER PRINCIPLE

People like Lisa and William are inspiring, but many more are like Amanda—unclear about what they personally value and what purpose leadership might serve in their own lives. If that's you too, new roles may just happen *to* you, whether you're ready or not.

Great employees like Amanda may find themselves in leadership roles that do not align with their strengths or personal goals simply because everyone ascribes to the idea that we must always be moving up. It's incredibly common. So common, there's a name for it—"The Peter principle."[28] The idea—that every employee tends to rise to his level of incompetence—was advanced by Canadian psychologist J. Lawrence Peter in his half-satirical book by the same name. We've all seen it happen: when an employee demonstrates competence and does well in a role, he's rewarded with a promotion. If he demonstrates competence and does well in the new role, he will be promoted again. This continues until the employee reaches his level of incompetence and his final promotion, where he will remain—one level above his own competence.

The Peter principle has been scientifically validated. David Burkas of Oral Roberts University explained it perfectly in a 1999 article:

> The Peter principle is more than just a satirical comment on large bureaucracy or a strange organizational phenomenon. It's a symptom of a culture that overvalued titles and undervalued being connected to the work you are best at. That our culture drives us away from roles in which we'd thrive all for the purpose of a better-looking business card. We're

---

[28] Laurence J. Peter and Raymond Hull, *The Peter Principle: Why Things Always Go Wrong* (New York: Harper Business, 2014).

subtly influenced to believe that more responsibility, bigger offices, and better-sounding titles are always better.[29]

The Peter principle happens, but it doesn't have to happen to you. You can avoid being promoted to the level of your own incompetence. If you pay attention to your "why"—why you do the work you do, why you want to be in leadership, and why you want to serve in a particular role—you will have a better filter through which to make decisions about your career. You won't be so easily enticed by what you "should" do, or the next shiny object you spy, whether that's more money or a bigger title.

With your eyes wide open, you'll be able to make decisions that are right for you. If there's an opportunity for you to move into something where you feel you can learn and progress, by all means, do it! I'll never discourage anyone from exploring something new, pushing themselves, and taking on bigger challenges. Life is too short not to. My wish for you is to simply be aware of your own strengths, motivations, and purpose.

WHY ASK WHY?

Part of loving leadership is knowing why you do it—your purpose. The word "purpose" gets thrown around so

---

[29] Alan Benson, Danielle Li and Kelly Shue, "Promotions and the Peter Principle," *NBER Working Paper*, no. 24343 (February 2018).

much these days, we might forget that it literally means the "reason something is done." The only way to be truly engaged, committed, and inspired in anything, especially leadership, is to have a clear connection to your purpose—your own personal "why." Remember, leadership is hard. If you don't have a real grip on your reason for doing it, the long hours, constant availability, difficult people, and growing to-do lists will leave you feeling overwhelmed and wondering what it's all for. I've had more than one person over the years walk into my office, shut the door, collapse on the nearest chair, and ask something along the lines of, "What the hell are we even doing here? I don't know if I'm coming or going, and I don't know if I can do it anymore. Why am I putting myself through this?!?"

If you aren't personally grounded in something bigger, you're also going to find yourself being jerked around by every organizational change, priority shift, and crisis that comes up. You'll find yourself at the mercy of everyone else's agenda, which is emotionally exhausting and unsustainable. And that's when the suffering can creep in.

Being connected to your work and having something personal to hang on to when the winds of change feel more like a tornado from hell can make all the difference to your sanity.

GETTING IN TUNE WITH YOUR "WHY"

Comedian Michael Jr. regularly takes time out of his stand-up routine to chat with his audience. He posts these "Break Times" on YouTube. In one episode, he randomly picked a man in the audience who turned out to be a music director. He told the guy, "Alright, sing me something." The man, Daryl, sang two stanzas of Amazing Grace. He did a great job. After all, it's what he does for a living. His voice was smooth and every note was perfect. The hymn sounded exactly the way it should if a music director was singing it.

Michael Jr. congratulated Daryl on an impressive rendition.

"Now," said Michael Jr.," I want you to sing it like you're at the funeral of your nephew who just got shot in the back in some random act of violence in the street. I want you to get down with it."

After a moment, Daryl started to sing. He found notes that weren't there before. His voice soared, drawing notes out and hitting all of the highs and lows and places in between. His intonation was different, and so was the feeling. People around him were on their feet, some were crying, and some came over to give him a hug. I'm pretty sure he saved somebody that day.

The song was the same and the words were the same. The only thing that was different was Daryl's "why." As Michael Jr. said, the song was perfectly fine the first time, but when Daryl connected with his "why," it gave the song a reason for being sung. The "why" made all the difference. (I encourage you to check it out.)[30]

---

30   Michael Jr., *Know Your Why*, https://www.youtube.com/watch?v=LZe5y2D6oYU.

FIGURE OUT YOUR *"WHY"*

Let's examine your "why." To make it easier, it can be broken down into two parts: *motivation* and *purpose*. Motivation is what you get to have, be, or do if you are in a leadership role. Purpose goes a level deeper, asking why what you get to have, be, or do matters to you.

I'll give you an example. When my sister started a very strict diet to lose ten pounds, I asked why she wanted to lose the weight. She said she liked the way she felt when she was ten pounds lighter. I pressed for more. Digging deeper, she realized losing the weight and feeling better was important to her because she'd be more energetic and able to be more active with her kids which she equated to being a better mom. The motivation for my sister's dieting was losing the ten pounds, but the deeper purpose for her was to be a better mom. Knowing both her motivation, what she gets to have, be, or do, and purpose, why that truly matters to her, connect her to something bigger than a diet and significantly improve her opportunity to be successful.

What is your motivation for becoming a leader? What is your purpose? Here are a couple of tools for you to explore:

- **Make a list**: Try listing out the things that energize you and then those things that leave you feeling drained. Consider the times you're having fun, as well as what drives you crazy. Don't hold anything back. Get it all on paper and then take some time to really connect the dots for yourself and identify common themes. What do you see and how do you feel about it? The simple act of thinking about why you want to be a leader and listing all the things that come to mind can provide some awareness about why you choose to lead.

- **Work with a coach**: I genuinely believe in the power of working with a strong thought partner to peel back the layers of "should," "could," and "supposed to" to figure out what's really driving your decisions. I've seen first-hand what can happen when leaders are able to stop struggling with themselves and start focusing on the influence and impact they want to have on something greater. That's why I'm writing this book for you. If we were coaching one-on-one, here are some of the things that I would ask you to consider and answer for yourself:
    - What motivates me? What do I get to have, be, or do as a leader?
    - What do I really love about the work I get to do now? Will I have more or less of that in a leadership role?
    - What am I doing when I feel like I'm at my best? Will I get to do more or less of that in a leadership role?
    - Why is what I get to have, be, or do through leadership important to me?

- If I could accomplish only one thing as a leader, what would it be?
- If I could accomplish only one thing as a person, what would it be?

Look for alignment, and, more importantly, any misalignment in your answers.

It doesn't matter *how* you clarify your "why" but it matters that you do. Because when you're able to connect your own reasons to your work, leadership or not, you'll be able to weather the challenges and find the joy so much more easily because you know why you're doing it. You will reek of personal commitment and confidence that comes from knowing this thing you do is connected to something greater than the to-do list, quarterly metrics, or strategic plans. It's hard because it matters. It matters to the people you lead, the organization you choose to serve, and, most importantly, it matters to you.

I hope you're nodding your head in agreement, but most of the time, this is the point where my corporately conditioned clients tell me I've got this all wrong. They'll tell me that leadership is all about selflessly serving others and putting the company's goals above your own. And to that I respectfully say—bullshit. While the idea of serving the organization above all is an extremely beneficial one for the company, that isn't how things really work.

Remember that work, at its core, is simply an exchange of time and talent for money. Only the human being doing the work can make it more than that. And for work to be more than a simple exchange for you, you must know what purpose it serves for you in your life. Then, and arguably only then, can you be emotionally connected to your work, your people, or your organization. In twenty years of working one-on-one with human beings serving at every level of leadership, I never once met an effective, inspiring, or memorable leader that couldn't articulate why their work was important to them on a personal level.

Once you've done the work to clarify your motivation and purpose, you should be pretty close to articulating your own work "why." It might be challenging—self-awareness usually is, but it can be powerful. The good news is that there's no right answer. It's not my place or anyone else's to tell you whether your "why" is good or bad. Some reasons may make leadership more challenging for you, but whatever it is, it's *your* reason. *Your* "why."

MONEY

What came up for you when you considered your own motivation and purpose for serving in a leadership role? Did money play into it? It did for more than half of the people in my straw poll. Lots of people take jobs for a bigger paycheck. I've done it. Early in my career, I took an

HR role solely for the money. It was one of the worst work experiences I have ever had, and that's saying something.

Don't worry if money is one of your motivators. After all, money is why most of us work, right? Making money is not a bad thing. If, however, money is your motivation, then you *have* to explore and identify what purpose money serves in your life. Sure, you want to have enough money to survive, but it probably serves a purpose beyond buying the basic necessities. Perhaps money will help you provide more security for your family than you had growing up and that's really important to you. Maybe you simply want to make loads of money because you like nice toys and big trips. Or maybe you have an expensive hobby that work allows you to fund. No wrong reason.

Just remember that if you're in it for the money, you still have to get your mind right about the challenges of leadership and commit to positively influencing and supporting those counting on you. That does not change whether you're in it for the money or the mission. If you try taking on a new leadership role *solely* for the money without connecting to a deeper personal "why," you're going to struggle and likely create some suffering in the process. Because there's simply not enough money in the world to compensate you for the challenges of leading other human beings if you don't find joy in it. Plus, if you're responsible for influencing other people to meet certain outcomes, you're going to have to motivate *them*. And making you rich isn't likely to motivate anyone. If you are only in it for the bucks, they will smell it from a mile away.

POWER

Maybe it's not money that floats your boat, but power. I urge you to tread carefully here. If your reason for becoming a leader is your attraction to the authority the position gives you, then you may find it difficult to effectively influence others to positive outcomes. Sometimes playing the power card does seem to work—there are studies indicating that a drive for power or authority is often present in successful leaders, especially at the top of the corporate hierarchy—but too much can look more like narcissism.

Power-hungry leaders are typically relentless in their pursuit of responsibility and leadership, discounting the fact that real power in modern leadership lies with followers. Long-term success is much more difficult to achieve when your quest for authority is entirely self-centered. Although it happens. I've worked for a couple of "successful" leaders who had no problem leaving a few bodies behind them on their way up. When your position and perks are your motivation, it's way too tempting to make decisions based on fear of losing your prime parking space or fancy title. So maybe just don't be that guy.

I admit that I spent much of the first half of my career trying to prove that I deserved the next title and the next level of responsibility. There were points early in my climb that I was so self-absorbed and focused on being "the boss" that I made some harmful decisions. Decisions that directly impacted the human beings around me. I had a very shallow "why" back then, and I didn't appreciate the impact I would have on others. I'm certainly not proud of the suffering that I caused even if it was unintentional. Regret is one of the most painful emotions to experience, and I don't want that for you or anyone else. Which is why I encourage all of my coaching clients, audiences, and you to take a minute to consider the responsibilities and think through why you want to be a leader.

THE "SHOULDS"

Money and power aside, some people fall into leadership roles with no "why" in mind at all. They do it because it feels like something they "should" do. Which is completely understandable given our societal push to climb, climb, climb. But anytime you find yourself making a decision because you feel like it's what you *should* do, you owe it to yourself to look deeper to figure out where that feeling is coming from. Whenever my clients tell me they feel like they should do something I share my personal acronym for should:

Stop
Handing
Over
Ur
Life's
Decisions

When you do something because you think you should, you are literally giving up the power to make the decision for yourself. You have to explore the source of that feeling and question why you believe it to be true. Being a leader is a big deal. As a leader, you'll have a lot of responsibility and make an important impact, so be sure you want it for yourself, not because society says it's the thing to do. Why is leadership the "thing to do" for you?

DESIRE TO INFLUENCE

Your reason for wanting to lead will be unique to you, and if you've put in the time to define that, you have my deepest respect. You might be wondering how others articulate their reasons, though. So here you go. If I've seen a common thread among the happier leaders I've coached, it's this: a genuine *want* and desire to positively influence other people.

As Jay Howard Sterling, Harvard business professor, wrote in a 1971 issue of the *Harvard Business Review*:

> Only those who have a strong desire to influence the performance of others and who get genuine satisfaction from doing so can learn to lead effectively. No leader is likely to learn how unless she really wants to take responsibility for the productivity of others and enjoys developing and motivating them to achieve better results.[31]

I agree. You have to have a strong desire to manage and influence others. You have to get genuine joy out of making a difference for and through others. If you've ever tried to make yourself love something that you really don't want to do, you know it doesn't work. You'll only suffer and cause suffering for others. If you want to love what you do, create joy, and have real impact, you have to clarify your "why" and choose for yourself, be it leadership or something else. If you've decided that leadership is right for you, then you've already done more than most leaders. Good leaders know why they lead. But great leaders know who they want to be.

TOUGH-LOVE QUESTIONS
NEW OR ASPIRING LEADER

In this chapter, you've learned how important it is to consciously decide if leadership is right for you.

---

[31] J. Sterling Livingston, "Myth of the Well-Educated Manager," *Harvard Business Review*, January 1971.

- So, why do you want to be a leader?

EXPERIENCED LEADER

It doesn't matter how you got here. You're in a leadership role and responsible for the productivity and outcomes of other human beings. Even now, you need to understand your "why."

- So, why do you want to continue to be a leader?

CHAPTER 4

YOUR LEADERSHIP, YOUR CONTEXT

Robert was a CEO looking to hire his operations leader. After several months of sourcing and screening qualified and experienced applicants, he and his team narrowed the pool to two. Each candidate had a unique personality and skillset that would add value to the team.

One of the candidates was a bit more mature, with a calm demeanor and years of experience in similar roles. The second candidate was more of a gamble. She, too, was very competent, but she was also enthusiastic and a great storyteller. She would be able to rally the team. However, she was still early in her career. Her confidence slightly pushed the boundaries of arrogance, and her enthusiasm had a touch of naiveté.

Robert was also early in his career, and upper-level management was encouraging him to be very wise in his decision. Although the decision was ultimately Robert's to make, his senior managers felt very strongly that he should bring in someone with more experience and maturity to supplement his lack of leadership experience.

Robert was torn over the decision. He had a vision of building a team that would be innovative and creative in the face of some big operational and market changes that were happening in his organization. And he felt strongly that the less experienced candidate would be the best and could help him accomplish the goals he'd set.

Robert's struggle was not over which candidate would be best. His struggle was whether to follow his instincts or the guidance of his more experienced advisors. He was internally conflicted over what he felt was the right decision for his team and what he was being told he should do. Remember what I said about "should"?

After working through all of the pros and cons of each candidate, I asked Robert who he wanted to be in his role as CEO. He said, "Obviously, I want to be me." I asked him, "Then what do *you* want to do?" He said, "I would hire the more enthusiastic candidate. She's what we need right now. I need creativity. I need someone who isn't brainwashed about how things have always been done, because we can't do what's already been done. We need fresh, innovative, and fairly aggressive ideas that will get this team progressing. We need to stop losing ground and start gaining very quickly."

Even though he was clear on the right hire, Robert was struggling because he didn't want to disappoint his senior leaders or make a mistake that might cost time or even his own credibility. At the same time, he knew that the experienced candidate was a safer choice. Even if he turned out to be wrong for the job, Robert's advisors couldn't be too hard on him since they were the ones who'd supported the hire.

I got it, but he was still struggling, so I asked again, "Who do you want to be in this role? Do you want to be a leader that makes safe decisions, relying heavily on the guidance and advice of your superiors? Or do you want to be the leader that thoughtfully considers the advice of others, evaluates the situation, assesses the risks and rewards, and then takes risks where appropriate while following your own instincts?"

Then, the zinger: "Which decision supports the leader that you wish to become?"

It took Robert five seconds to decide. He already knew. He didn't take this position with this organization undergoing so much change because he wanted to be a "safe leader." He also didn't want to be a foolish leader, but he didn't think he was.

Instead, he said, "I want to be a leader that makes decisions based on what's right for our team right now. I don't want to be the guy that makes the decisions that are safest for me. I want to do what I believe is best for our people, even when it seems a little risky. That's the type of leader and person I want to be."

He believed in his decision.

WHO ARE YOU?

As children, we're often asked *what* we want to be when we grow up. It's really the first interview question we're asked and it starts somewhere around the age of five or six. Our answer in kindergarten doesn't hold much weight, but we're expected to have a pretty good idea of what we want to be by the time we're seventeen or eighteen years old. But the more important question is the one we are rarely, if ever, asked:

Who do you want to be?

Epictetus, a Greek philosopher, posed the question more pointedly: "Who *exactly* do you want to be? If you wish to be an extraordinary person, if you wish to be wise, then you should explicitly identify the kind of person that you aspire to become."

As Stephen Covey says, "People can't live with change if there's not a changeless core inside them. The key to the ability to change is a changeless sense of who you are, what you are about and what you value."

Knowing who you want to be as a leader requires getting clear on who you are as a person, understanding your self-worth, and defining your own personal values.

YOU ARE MORE THAN A JOB TITLE

Our leader-loving society assumes that leaders have certain essential qualities and characteristics, yet few can agree what those characteristics are. Each college you apply to, company you interview with, and supervisor you ask for a promotion will have unique ideas about what makes a leader a leader.

That's a problem, because if you aren't clear on who you want to be and the values that are most important to you, you may find yourself trying to be the person each of them expects you *should* be.

In our culture we tend to place a lot of value on what we

do and what we have. Think about it. When we meet someone new, we get their name then immediately ask, "So, what do you do?" Do we actually want to know what they do all day at work? No. We're angling for another piece of information—their job title. That piece of information is important in our culture, where "what you do" defines us to a great extent. Many of us are so tied to our work that our titles become who we are.

Moving beyond a work-based definition of ourselves can be very challenging. When I ask my coaching clients to decide who they want to be, it almost always throws them for a loop. They'll sputter a few incoherent sentences trying to come up with the "right" answer before giving up and asking me what exactly I mean by *who*. It's hard to answer right away, because it's not something we're often asked to consider. Digging for the answer can be challenging, too, because I'm really asking them to dive deeper than *what* they do, deeper than the description on their business card.

I'm going to challenge you the same way. Who are you if you aren't wearing a suit, making bank every two weeks, or buying the biggest, latest, and greatest thing? Don't get me wrong, the suit, the money, and the things can be quite satisfying. But these external measures of societal success cannot define the core of a person.

When I first left my corporate HR role, I struggled. If I

wasn't Angie, HR exec, then who was I? What value did I have if I no longer valued a title the rest of the world deemed important? It was an unexpectedly painful time. For the first few months I felt like a loser. When someone would ask me, "what do you do?" I'd struggle to spit out something that would seem respectable and worthy. In the beginning I'd try too hard and end up saying a lot of nothing, like "I'm the Chief Engagement Officer of my own small business. But it's not really a business yet because I'm still trying to figure out what I sell and stuff like that—ya know. " And nothing kills a conversation like saying "I'm exploring my options right now." That one was often met with "Oh. Good for you. Hey, isn't that Sally? Please excuse me. Good luck." (Quickly exit stage left.)

Turns out the only thing worse than not having a formal title is being unsure of what you're actually doing or going to do next. Maybe people are afraid uncertainty is contagious. Or maybe they thought that I was going to hit them up for a job, I don't know. I finally settled on "I'm a consultant" because everyone buys that one, right? And it did match the work I was doing. But the truth was that I was struggling with my own identity because I had attached so much of who I was to my work. Until my daughter was born, my work had been my life.

Although it was quite painful at the time, I'm so grateful now for that first year of uncertainty because I was forced to learn—really learn—that I was more than my job title. And you are, too. You are so much more than John, Director of Sales, or Lisa, Unit Manager. You are more than the number of zeroes on your paycheck. You are first and foremost a human being with a unique set of strengths, talents, and characteristics worthy in your own right, title or no title, Mercedes or Chevy. You may be a parent, a sibling, a spouse, a friend, a creator, an executor, a survivor, an explorer, a learner, a truth-teller, a seer, and a million other things. You are never just one thing. On top of that, you are always becoming something new, changed, and different with each decision you make and every experience you have.

Right about now, you may be wondering what any of this woo-woo has to do with leadership? Stick with me. The source of your self-worth is important because that's what guides your decisions about whether—and how—to pursue leadership opportunities. If your value or self-worth depends on what you *do* or what you *have*, then you may find yourself climbing ladders simply to prove your worth to the rest of the world and maybe yourself. Climbing, climbing, climbing only to find that you aren't as happy or fulfilled at the top as you had hoped. When you're sure of *who* you are, beyond what you do, then you're truly free to choose what is right for you. That has a nice ring to it.

WORK, LIFE, AND YOU

I'm not saying that what you do doesn't matter. It does!

Psychologists have long celebrated the power of meaningful work to improve people's self-esteem. It's true that doing work that matters to you almost always adds to your sense of personal self-worth, but the demands of today's workplace—and especially the increasing demands of leadership—can also undermine it. If you're in a role that is always on, always driving for more, and always taking the heat, you can easily begin to feel inadequate, incompetent, or simply not good enough to keep up with the increasing demands. All things that can leave you feeling devalued. When you feel that way, you will struggle, create suffering for yourself and others, and stop growing as a leader. The antidote? Get grounded in the knowledge that work is simply a part of your life and neither your successes or failures at work define the whole of it.

Simple, right? I know; it's simple in theory, but hard as hell to practice. Work is such a huge part of our lives, and it does provide the means for getting the things we need and want. Societal standards celebrating work are pretty well ingrained. I get it. And this isn't a psychology book, so I won't pretend to offer you the tools for discovering the meaning of life.

What I will offer you is a reminder that you are a walking, talking miracle of the universe. Statistically speaking the odds of you being you are somewhere between 1 in 400 trillion and 1 in $10^{2,685,000}$ (aka infinitely tiny odds), depending on who you ask.[32]

Do you think the universe spat you out with those odds so that you could grow up to become "You—Shift Supervisor at Makememoremoney Corp." No! You were made to be "You—quick thinking, problem-solving, people loving, organized, responsible, funny, master gardening, intelligent, articulate, (add your own unique skills and qualities here) human being who currently earns a living bringing all that cool stuff to Makememoremoney Corp. as a Shift Supervisor." See the difference?

If your sense of identity is tied up in your title, then you are quite literally putting your self-worth in the hands of an entity that is designed to exist with or without you. Not because organizations are bad—remember, I'm not anti-company; I'm pro-you—but because they are, by design, self-sustaining entities that must shift, shrink, and expand with market and other external conditions. You must be able to stand firm in who you are *as a person* to ride those ups and downs without losing yourself.

The increasing pace of change and amped up expectations

---

[32] Dina Spector, "The Odds of You Being Alive are Incredibly Small," *Business Insider*, June 11, 2012, https://www.businessinsider.com/infographic-the-odds-of-being-alive-2012-6.

aren't just concepts. They're real. As a leader, that can be exciting: you'll have a front-row seat to the unimaginable innovation and industry-shifting disruption occurring in the workforce today. It can also be overwhelming: the rise in work-related stress, anxiety, and depression that accompanies these changes is no joke.[33] You'll be responsible for guiding other people through those ups and downs as well, which, in turn, can cause more stress for you. If you live and die by your success or failure at work, you may end up a hyper-focused, overly-intense leader who is hard, if not impossible, to work with. You don't want to be that person. To be effective, influential, and sane, you need to think enough of yourself not to take it all too personally.

PERSONAL VALUES

Part of defining who you are and if you want to be a leader is defining your personal values or the things that you believe are most important or desirable to you individually. Your personal values are the principles or core beliefs you hold about right and wrong and how things ought to be in your life and the world around you. You believe in these things so wholeheartedly that you are willing to stand up or fight for them. Your personal values often serve as your internal compass or guide—whether you recognize them or not.

---

[33] "Workplace Stress," *The American Institute of Stress*, https://www.stress.org/workplace-stress/.

Many of our deeply held beliefs about what is important are instilled in us as children by our parents and the dominant values of the society within which we live. In other words, many of our values are ideals impressed upon us by others as we grow up. And those values influence the decisions we make around relationships, parenting, careers, and other big decisions that impact the direction of our lives.

The challenge with other people's values is that, well... they're other people's values. Yet many of us go through life without ever really questioning what we personally value most and why. That's why we can end up building careers or lives that don't quite feel like our own. We can so easily find ourselves doing what we think we should do, rather than what really lights us up. We go with the societal flow and even adopt other's ideas of success, which is the perfect recipe for suffering. Especially in leadership.

WHEN SOMETHING DOESN'T FEEL RIGHT

To get clear about your values, it's helpful to consider moments when something doesn't feel right. Maybe you've taken an action, as instructed, but it feels wrong. Or maybe you've observed an activity that goes against your beliefs. That's called "misalignment." When there's misalignment, you know it, even if you can't articulate it—something just doesn't feel right.

Recognizing misalignment is important, because one of the most common symptoms of unhappiness, dissatisfaction, or disengagement with work among the leaders that I've worked with is exactly this: misalignment of values and actions.

Believe me, I know. It happened to me some years ago, long before I had done any research on values, let alone defined my own. I was part of the leadership team at a faith-based organization, leading the process of evaluating our outsourced support services. Collectively, we had decided to terminate a contract with one of our long-term vendors and offer employment to the people who had really become part of our team. The hiccup was a clause in the contract stating that my organization would have to pay a hefty fee for the privilege of hiring those employees.

That made sense. After all, we originally agreed to the terms of the contract. Our representative signed the contract. We knew that if we terminated, we'd be liable for the fee. Yet I found myself talking to attorneys and attending secret meetings with our senior leaders, trying to find a way to terminate the contract without paying the fee. By the time we finished two confidential meetings on the matter and were an hour into a third call, I was starting to stew a little. Something didn't feel right.

I finally grew so frustrated I had to speak up. I said, "What we are doing doesn't feel very aligned with who we say we are as an organization. We signed that contract knowing that if we wanted out of it at some point, these would be the terms. And we're spending a lot of time and resources trying to figure out how *not* to comply. I'm certain that we would expect the vendor to comply with the terms of the agreement if they wanted to terminate. And I'm also pretty sure that we would be open to discussions with them about possible concessions. Have we even had a discussion with the vendor to ask if they would be willing to concede the fee?" The answer was a resounding no. We hadn't wanted to tip them off to the fact that we were terminating until we figured out if we could get around the fee.

What were we doing? We were a faith-based organization committed to upholding certain organizational values—respect, integrity, compassion, and excellence! And here we were, trying to finagle the termination to avoid the particular terms we no longer wished to adhere to. We were violating at least two of our own stated organizational values. We were definitely not demonstrating respect for the vendor, nor operating with integrity. I didn't have a conscious epiphany that my personal values were being violated. I just knew that something didn't feel right.

As a result of our frank discussion, we wound up having a direct conversation with the vendor. We explained why we were terminating the contract and presented our case for keeping the employees. After some open and honest negotiations they conceded the fee, the employees got to keep their jobs, and everyone was able to walk away feeling respected.

No organization is perfect. Organizations may espouse well-intentioned values and mission statements, like ours did, but I can promise you, just as sure as I'm writing this book for you, you will come face to face with some questionable influencers and decisions. To cope, you must have a strong sense of your own foundational principles. Without them you can quickly find yourself pulled knee-deep into someone else's ethical dilemma. As a leader you'll need to be able to remain grounded in your values, not only for your own emotional stability, but for the sake of your team as well.

Misalignment of values and actions can be a source of suffering. Because personal values run deep, people will struggle to do, say, or support anything that feels like a threat or challenge to their values, which can take a lot out of them, especially if they don't recognize exactly what's happening. If your gut is telling you something, but you can't pinpoint it, you may just go along with it, do your job, and try to meet expectations or keep the boss happy, but you'll probably find yourself feeling resistant, resentful, or even angry about it. And those feelings can become destructive.

That said, none of us is going to be 100 percent in agreement with every single operational decision. As a leader, you will definitely face times when you need to implement a program or take some action that you do not necessarily agree with. That's part of the job. But you'll need to be able to connect those actions to the greater purpose with which you are aligned if you hope to positively motivate and influence your team.

And sometimes you have to speak up. If I hadn't spoken up about the contract negotiations, I would have been stressed out, conflicted, and disappointed in my colleagues. I would've taken the stress home with me, eaten a whole bag of potato chips, and been less present with my family. I would have been thinking about the call, stewing over how it didn't feel right and growing frustrated with people who had no idea about my concerns. Sounds a lot like disengagement, right?

It turns out that alignment of values is one of the top ten drivers of engagement *and* disengagement. It's so important at work that highly engaged employees rank it as one of the top contributors to why they're able to connect with their organization.[34] And a lack of alignment between company values and actions—or misalignment—

---

34 "What Causes Employee Disengagement?" *Custom Insight*, https://www.custominsight.com/employee-engagement-survey/research-employee-disengagement.asp.

is one of the top reasons that disengaged employees give for being disconnected.

Part of a leader's role is to help people make a personal connection to the work they're doing. To be effective in making this connection for others, you must be able to make it for yourself. Do that and you will fulfill one of the greatest responsibilities of a leader—connecting people to the big picture, the greater mission of the organization. People, at every level, need to know what they're trying to accomplish, understand why the work they do matters, and recognize how it contributes to that bigger picture.

DEFINING YOUR PERSONAL VALUES

What are your personal values?

I know, defining your personal values sounds like an ominous task, but it is simply the act of bringing awareness to those things that you value and desire to have most in your life. You can do this.

One caveat: when you do this exercise, try not to compare your values to others or list those that you think you should value. If they aren't yours, they aren't yours. No judgment here. Defining your values is not an exercise of right or wrong. There is only alignment or misalignment.

STEP 1

On a piece of paper, write out every core value that comes to mind. Below is a short list to help you get started. There are more comprehensive lists online if choosing from a larger bank of words is easier.

Achievement	Adventure	Accountability	Attractiveness	Autonomy
Balance	Best	Boldness	Calmness	Caring
Challenge	Community	Control	Creativity	Curiosity
Daring	Decisiveness	Dependability	Diversity	Empathy
Encouragement	Enthusiasm	Excellence	Fairness	Family
Friendship	Flexibility	Freedom	Fun	Generosity
Growth	Happiness	Health	Honesty	Humor
Inclusiveness	Independence	Individuality	Innovation	Intelligence
Intuition	Learning	Love	Loyalty	Making a difference
Originality	Professionalism	Risk taking	Recognition	Teaching
Teamwork	Spirituality	Wisdom	Wealth	Well-being

STEP 2

Take all of the words that you've come up with and group them together into four or five categories that make sense to you. Then choose the word from each grouping that best represents that category. See? Not so hard. You should now have a pretty good idea of the top values in your life.

Knowing your values will help you to build a life and

career grounded in what's really important to you. It won't magically change anything about your workplace or the world around you, but it gives you the self-awareness you need to handle those situations where you have that feeling in your gut that you can't quite pinpoint. When you experience prolonged frustration or resentfulness, you'll recognize where those feelings might be coming from. Express them in your leadership and you will build credibility and trust with your people.

Knowing your values doesn't mean they're written in stone, though. While core values typically remain pretty stable, the context may change. Remember my client Susan from Chapter 1—the one daydreaming about a car wreck to skip work? Two of the things she valued most in her work were challenge and success. After her children were born, these core values didn't necessarily change, but she defined success differently. It was no longer about money and status. Success, after her boys were born, meant striking a balance between the work she enjoyed doing and being present with her children. She ended up fantasizing about time off from work, whatever the cost, because her new definition of success no longer aligned with her old work situation. After getting clear on her new definition of success, she could pinpoint the problem. She hadn't stopped enjoying her accounting work, but the travel and the client load she carried were rubbing right up against her value of balance. Within a few months she was able to find a new position within her sons' school district that was a perfect fit. She still had a ton of work and loads of responsibility, but she didn't have to travel, and she got the bonus of knowing that every hour of work she put in contributed directly to the education system her children were a part of.

Same values, different context. As you experience significant life changes, you'll want to revisit your values list, look for misalignment, and make adjustments where needed.

DECIDING WHO YOU WANT TO BE AS A LEADER

You've gotten clear on the source of your self-worth and defined your own personal values. Now, let's pour all that information into the context of leadership and paint a clear picture of the leader that you intend to be. Your intentions will drive your behavior. Your behaviors will drive your leadership.

First, think of the worst leader you ever worked with. I bet you remember his name, the date you met him, even what you were wearing when you finally quit. You probably vowed never to be that guy. What was it about him that made him difficult to work for? What behaviors, habits, and traits drove you bananas or made it hard for you to be effective under his leadership?

Second, think about a leader you admire. What are the traits that you most admire or respect about this person? Why do you respect those things? What are the underlying principles and values that make them admirable?

Finally, consider what type of leader *you* want to be. List out the characteristics and the traits that you most want to demonstrate in your leadership. What do you want people to see in your leadership?

> **WALKING YOUR "WHY"**
>
> Alignment between your work and your values produces satisfaction, fulfillment, and a sense of happiness—and quite possibly even engagement, if you choose. With every decision you'll be able to ask, does this decision support the person I want to be and align with what's most important to me?
>
> In Chapter 3 we talked about getting clear on why leadership is important to you and what purpose serving others serves for you. Understanding your personal values allows you to marry all of those things together when it comes to making decisions and taking action.
>
> Susan David, Harvard Psychology Professor, says it best in her book *Emotional Agility*:
>
> "Walking your why is the art of living by your own personal set of values."

You've done a lot of the hard work. Things will change and shift over time, and you have to be prepared to move with them and take the initiative to be the best leader possible. Read on in the next chapter and own your shift!

TOUGH-LOVE QUESTIONS

NEW OR ASPIRING LEADER

Consider how serving in a leadership role supports your personal core values and answer the following questions.

- What areas of leadership align well with what's important to you?
- What areas do you need to be mindful of that have the potential for misalignment?

EXPERIENCED LEADER

Consider your current leadership beliefs, practices, and behaviors as you answer the following questions.

- Is there anything expected or required of you in your current leadership role that feels like it goes against the grain a little for you?
- What is it about that expectation, action, or behavior that doesn't feel right?
- What are some ways you could bring those things into alignment with your own values and still accomplish the objective?

CHAPTER 5

OWN YOUR OWN SHIFT

Taylor had a long tenure with the hospital she worked for, starting out as a nurse assistant and working her way up as a nurse. She eventually moved into a position as director of patient experience.

The most important aspects of Taylor's job were problem-solving, addressing complaints, and handling difficult guest relations. She was exceptional at being the kind face of the hospital when something was going wrong. She was friendly, compassionate, and understanding with patients as well as her peers. Taylor's senior leadership got to know her in this role and recognized how good she was at it.

Taylor's goals, however, did not end with this position. She had her sights set on a senior level leadership role with greater leadership and operations responsibility. She applied for a number of positions that came open and was told that she needed a master's degree, which she was working on. Once she received her degree, however, she was still denied promotions. Her interviewers thought it was too much of a stretch for Taylor to move into that level of leadership because they believed it demanded a more aggressive and direct personality.

Taylor continued to apply. I was privy to the back-office conversations about Taylor and it was pretty clear to me that she would never be given the opportunity she was seeking. It just wasn't going to happen. Management simply did not see the "strength" they thought she needed to have to be in the leadership role. In their minds, Taylor was the friendly, outgoing "patient experience person."

Taylor continued to develop herself. She gained as much experience and exposure as she could in the organization related to clinical leadership. She joined committees and put herself in the middle of projects that allowed her to exercise the necessary skills and be seen in a different light. But that didn't happen. Ultimately, Taylor had to leave the organization to reach her goal. She was hired as an assistant chief nursing officer in a much larger health care system, a position she'd been denied in the previous organization.

Taylor's story is not an isolated one. You've probably

known someone who can't seem to get the attention of their leaders no matter how hard they work. Or maybe they made that one mistake years ago that seems to be holding them back still no matter how much exceptional work they've done since then. Right or wrong, it happens.

If Taylor had waited for her next-level leaders to see her differently or to give her the opportunity that she wanted, she may not have ever reached her goal. Her bosses weren't jerks, they were just imperfect human beings who had gotten to know her in a particular role. And they had their own ideas about the personality traits needed to be a successful leader—based largely on their experience in their context. And no matter how idealistically we paint the picture of perfect leadership, leaders are people. People who get it wrong sometimes.

The most important part of Taylor's story, however, is that Taylor took ownership of her career. She didn't wait to be tapped on the shoulder. Instead, she owned her career growth. She decided what she wanted, figured out what she needed to do, and then took all of the steps to get there. And so can you! You don't have to wait to be identified as leadership material, a high-potential employee, or a rising star. You don't have to stay pigeonholed or accept the narrow opinions of others regarding your capabilities or career trajectory. But what you do have to do is own your own shift.

OWNING YOUR ENGAGEMENT

Shift is defined by Merriam Webster as a change in emphasis, judgment, or attitude; a change in direction. Owning your own shift is about taking control of more than just the direction of your career. It means that you take responsibility for yourself in every aspect of work. When you own your own shift, you understand the importance of defining success for yourself, being the master of your own growth and development, and taking charge of your professional future. It also means that you take responsibility for your own personal engagement in your work.

Shift happens. (Sorry, I couldn't resist.) As we've covered in previous chapters, and as you are likely experiencing, everything we know about traditional work is changing. And it's changing fast. Disruption and exponential change have become the norm in practically every industry. Entire jobs are being modified or eliminated due to advancements in technology, including the use of artificial intelligence. Company structures are changing to support the rise in freelance, contract, and remote workers. And the average length of employment with any particular company is three to five years.[35]

This much change happening this quickly all around us

---

[35] Bureau of Labor Statistics, "Employee Tenure Summary," *Economic News Release*, September 20, 2018, https://www.bls.gov/news.release/tenure.nr0.htm.

can make it hard to stay engaged. It would be perfectly understandable if you were tempted to disengage; after all, it doesn't feel like there's much to hang on to. Unfortunately, that's a pretty miserable place to be—trust me. Instead of defaulting to disengagement, you must make a choice. Engagement can be a choice just as much as disengagement. You get to choose!

I can tell that disengagement isn't your style though. You're the type of person who wants to make a difference, and you recognize that change isn't personal—it just is. And as hard as it may be, you are going to maintain control over the one thing you always have control of in *every single situation*—you. You recognize that no one else is responsible for your decisions, your attitude, or your engagement. It's clear to you that the "company" cannot fulfill you. You have to take responsibility for your own choices, your attitude, and your behaviors because they are all, in fact, yours.

Owning your own engagement means that you maintain a level of self-awareness around how *you're* feeling at and about work. It means checking in with yourself first to assess how *you're* responding to leadership turnover, big strategy shifts, and frequent changes that upend the way you do things. It also means that you are responsible for the way that you react to other people. One of the greatest powers that you have as a human is the ability to decide, for yourself, how you will react or respond to any person in any situation. As Viktor Frankl said in *Man's Search For Meaning*, "The one thing you can't take away from me is the way I choose to respond to what you do to me."

We don't always own that. I cannot tell you how many times I've had adult professionals enter my office with the words "He started it." No. You are responsible for you. You learned this one in kindergarten and it is just as important now as it was then, if not more. Allowing any person or situation to reduce you to a level of behavior that does not reflect your own values or integrity is a choice. It is a choice to give away personal power and an expression of poor self-control. Personally, you are going to be tested on this principle time and time again. As a leader, your choices will directly impact your ability to influence others.

Choosing your reaction in difficult situations is definitely easier said than done. I've screwed it up more times than I care to admit. Like the time I let an angry employee draw me so far into an argument that I actually let a cuss word fly out—in a department meeting! Luckily this was very early in my career and the guy had pissed off everyone in the room, including my boss. But I was still held accountable for my decision to respond the way I did. And you will be too.

The people who choose to follow you will always be watching how you react to anything and everything. They won't expect you to be perfect any more than you expect your boss to be perfect. But they'll need consistency and stability from you. And if you're losing your shit every time a new process rolls out or someone pushes your buttons, you won't be demonstrating either. This will cause you to suffer and ultimately create suffering for those around you.

When you own your own shift, you make the intentional decision not to give your joy over to change or shifting strategies. You can choose not to chime in with the complainers or the passive-aggressives, or let Steve in accounting drive you to bad behavior no matter how many times he kicks your expense reports back to you.

And you sure as heck are not going to leave your goals and professional development in the hands of someone that may not be around in a couple of years. You have to take ownership of your own goals and development. Establishing solid relationships and networks is as important today as it has ever been, but relying on good relationships with key leaders to gain the recognition and support you need to grow may not the best strategy anymore, as those leaders are moving on more quickly these days.

LEARNING NEVER STOPS

Loving leadership is a long-term gig. No matter how easy or inspirational we make it seem, leadership is hard and it is constantly evolving. You never get it all figured out. You just don't. The simple truth is that nothing is the same today as it was ten years ago, and in a few years, nothing will be the same as it is now.

The learning never stops even for seasoned leaders. Unfortunately, the higher you go, the less discretionary time you may have for formal learning. And even worse, seasoned leaders can often feel like they're supposed to know everything by the time they reach a certain level. But the really smart ones understand that continued learning, especially now, is a sign of strength, not weakness.

New leaders often operate under the myth that they have to immediately be good—if not great—at leadership. They feel a tremendous amount of anxiety and stress to perform perfectly, right away, in a role that in reality takes time to learn. One of the best gifts you can give yourself as a leader is to cut yourself some slack. Accept that this thing is hard and that you'll always be learning. That acknowledgment alone could save you days, months, even years of doubting and questioning your competence or fit. It could free you from constantly worrying about screwing something up. Instead, you'll expect yourself to make mistakes and recognize them for the invaluable learning that they are.

Pretending you have it all figured out does a disservice to you and your people. If you can't get comfortable with not knowing, then you will always be looking for the "right" answer or solution and you may miss out on the *best* answer which might not look anything like the "right" one. Showing up with a learner's mindset, however, and acknowledging that you don't know it all, gives the people around you permission to do the same. When people feel free to explore, try, and learn (versus fail) without judgment, then creativity will flourish. And creativity is essential when change is the name of the game.

LEADERSHIP TRAINING

The next gift that I can offer you in your journey is to get real with you about one of the greatest challenges to leaders and good leadership in general—leadership training.

In Chapter 1, we discussed the main difficulty of defining leadership—it's contextual. It is dependent upon the environment, the culture, the situation, the needs, and the desires of the followers. Unfortunately, much leadership training operates under an assumption that good leadership is the same in every context and that it can be taught the same way to large groups of people regardless of individual strengths, opportunities, personality quirks, etc.

This kills me. We can't define leadership but we can teach it to everyone, the same way, in every setting? That can't be right. No wonder new leaders find themselves confused and overwhelmed. It's not at all surprising to me when new leaders share that they aren't sure how exactly to *do* all that great leadership stuff they've heard about in the context of their actual crazy work environment, with their old-school boss who still uses the term "chain-of-command." Or how to practice someone else's ideas of great leadership without coming off like a stuffed shirt.

But that's what the leadership training industry sells. (Remember Barbara Kellerman's quote: "Teaching *how* to lead is where the money is.") It's a multibillion-dollar industry predominantly catering to organizations, so when they sell training solutions guaranteed to make you a more productive, highly effective, and engaged leader, they are not talking about what's best for you; they sell what's best for the organization. (Never mind that many of the solutions don't work; we've seen that engagement rates have remained stagnant for more than fifteen years.)

Of course, the programs don't offer the exact same thing. Each leadership guru, expert, and training organization has a unique prescription for "successful" leadership. And with so many solutions and best practices out there you will undoubtedly find yourself subjected to a number of different leadership training programs, ideals, and models throughout your journey. You'll get checklists, scripts to follow, exercises to work through, and tasks to complete.

It seems great. You go to a leadership training program and get much-needed time away from the grind to learn this year's best practice. You get excited, motivated, and fired up. Finally, a leadership solution to make this gig easier! Whoop whoop! You won't even check your email, because you don't want anything to kill your training-day buzz. And you'll sleep soundly that night knowing you have everything you need to slay it tomorrow.

And then, you'll roll up to work the next day with a smile on your face and a pep in your step. Today, you are equipped. You now know that your leadership spirit animal is a lion and you are ready to roar. (Seriously, I've been to that training, too.) With checklists and scripts in hand, you make it about ten steps in the door and run smack dab into Jamie—the single most challenging employee on the planet. She's not happy with the new schedule and she's been waiting all morning with several other employees to talk to you about it—right now. Then your boss, whose spirit animal is a bear, yells across the room to you, even though you just yesterday learned yelling was not respectful behavior. He's yelling about the two reports he'd asked you about during the lunch break at yesterday's training. It's 8:15 a.m. Where are they? Your scripts aren't calming Jamie, you don't have an answer for your boss, and you spot an applicant waiting in the lobby for an interview. Just like that, your buzz is gone. By the end of the week, the training manual has been ever-so-neatly displayed on your miniature bookshelf alongside the previous years' training binders.

Does that sound at all familiar?

I'm not judging your company, the training organization, or even your boss. The truth is that leadership, though easy to teach in theory, is actually very challenging to teach in context. Leadership doesn't give a poo about your checklist; it is chaotic, emotional, and messy. That's why self-awareness is so incredibly important.

Listen, I'd love nothing more than to develop and teach a three-step, cookie-cutter program that would lead us all to leadership excellence. I'd be making bank—big bank—if only I could concede the notion that there's one simple way to become a masterful leader. Because that's what most organizations, and people, want to hear. Whether it works or not. Just tell us exactly *how* to be great.

The thing is, it's just not true. Learning to lead is like learning anything else. It's personal.

To get the most out of any training you attend, bring with you all of the self-awareness you've generated about who you are (personality and quirks included), your knowledge of your strengths, your opportunities, and where you are on your individual journey. Because you've done the personal work, you'll be able to apply your own context and individual situation to any training you receive. You'll be equipped to filter out the things that aren't applicable to you and take away only what's valuable for you. You don't have to jump completely into someone else's box only to later find out it doesn't work for you. Tools and insights are important for sure, but the thing that is going to make you a good leader is the thing that makes you *you*. No theory can cover the quirkiness or coolness that you as an individual bring to your leadership role.

The real learning, of course, happens in the doing. Be willing to experiment and see what works for you and for your team. Use what's effective for your style and personality. The absolute best thing you can do to support your own development, personally and professionally, is to remain open and recognize there's always something to learn in everything.

LEARNING BY EXPERIENCE

Experience is called the "best teacher" for a reason! You could hold multiple degrees, read a book a day, and still not be prepared for all of the curveballs you'll face as a leader. When it comes to dealing with people and employee relations, textbooks and scripts simply cannot provide all the answers. Leaders spend a lot of time managing in the gray area and much of what you'll find there won't necessarily correspond to the black and white pages of a book.

Learning through experience can be messy. You will fail at some things. That's okay when you're starting out. I know, you probably won't think it's okay. If you're like many people stepping into a leadership role, you probably compare yourself to leaders with ten to fifteen more years of experience who have been through many challenges you've yet to encounter. You aren't there yet, so give yourself a break. You can't expect to transition from a team player to coach with the click of an email announcement, no matter how enthusiastically your organization expresses their faith in your abilities.

Take the advice my mentor gave me after a speaking event where I felt like I had totally bombed. I had only been at it professionally for about six months, but I was completely discouraged and disappointed in myself. My mentor was having none of it. She said, "You're being ridiculous. You're just getting started, and you're expecting to be great, but you have to earn the right to be great. You have to screw it up a few times, survive those times, learn from those times, and get better because of them. Get a few scars. Then you can expect to be a great speaker, but you haven't earned that yet."

One of the most important things for you to remember as a new leader (and, for that matter, as an experienced leader) is that you're human. You will make mistakes. You're going to say the wrong thing in a meeting. You're going to get overly emotional in a crucial coaching conversation with an employee. You're going to miss a deadline (or two). You're going to send the email you should have waited to write until after you cooled off. And then you may even send that email to the wrong person or possibly the entire company. Not that any of that has ever happened to me. If you are actually doing anything, you're going to make the occasional mistake. It's just part of the deal. You just have to stay away from that awful f-word, failure, and keep perspective.

After you mess up a few things, apply some self-awareness and grow from it. You will learn to trust yourself over time. You know how to make good decisions even if you sometimes make mistakes. Mistakes are part of the process of becoming great at what you do. Listen to your gut feelings and trust that you are moving in the right direction.

WORKING WITH A COACH OR MENTOR

One way to fast track your own leadership development is to work with a coach or mentor. True coaching is a partnership with someone who gives you the space to work through issues by challenging some deep-seated beliefs you may have about yourself, or the world in general, that don't serve you. A coach can help you identify your blind spots and tap into the massive amount of potential you already have.

Working with a coach is like spending thirty minutes with a golf pro rather than hitting a thousand golf balls on your own. If it's just you, your clubs, and your jacked-up swing out there, it won't matter how many balls you hit; you're unlikely to improve. But a golf pro can take one look at you and see what you can't see for yourself—maybe you're not properly aligned with your target. Give her thirty minutes a week for a few months and you'll fix that hitch, sharpen up the rest of your swing, and improve your score in a fraction of the time, and suffering, of doing it on your own. A good leadership coach is to a leader what the golf pro is to the golfer. The insight, perspective, and experience that a coach can share could save you years of suffering.

Engaging with a mentor can also help you accelerate your career growth. Mentors can help you gain perspective. They know where the big potholes are; their years of experience allow them to show you where they are, keep you from stepping in them, or help you get out of one after you've fallen in. Your mentor has been there, done it, and survived to teach about it.

There really are few things more valuable to a new leader than the wisdom and experience of someone who's been, more or less, where you are in your leadership journey. A mentor offers two of the most precious gifts any of us have: wisdom and time. So if you find a good mentor, learn all you can from them and be sure to let them know you appreciate the value they are sharing with you. The best mentoring relationships are reciprocal—often, your mentor gets as much out of the exchange as you do. Being recognized for what they have to teach is very satisfying, and it's happening more often today, especially in multi-generational workplaces.

Mentoring can be a really useful development strategy, but one thing to remember is that you are getting only a single perspective from each mentor. That perspective may be helpful, but do keep in mind you are only hearing your mentor's ideas and philosophies as developed through their experience, personality, and skills. As with any training, you can use your self-awareness as a filter to discern the valuable nuggets. Leave the things that don't feel like you. You don't have to adopt your mentor's entire approach any more than you have to adopt a single method of training or leadership theory.

Mentors can also be wrong. Early in my career, about five years in, I got to serve as a mentor to a brand new recruiter in my organization. Debbie was a natural. She was very good in the recruiting role and she loved it. Not surprisingly, she had bigger goals. She started talking about becoming an HR generalist only a few months after being hired. The recruiter job was her first experience in HR, yet she expected to leap from being a recruiter to a generalist which required a much broader knowledge of HR with no prior experience.

My advice to Debbie was that she needed to get several more years of experience, take some additional courses, take the certification test and get certified *before* she considered such a move. I told her there was no way she was ready to make the move she was thinking about.

I was completely wrong.

My advice to Debbie was not mal-intended. I knew she was talented and would perform well as a generalist. I gave her the advice that was probably given to me and reflected my particular experiences up to that point in my own career journey. Luckily, Debbie didn't follow my advice.

She respectfully listened to what I had to say, took what she needed from it, and then did exactly what she wanted to do. She bought a book, studied for the test, and got that certification within a few months. She spent the next year or so getting as much experience as she could, getting involved in as many real-time situations as possible and asking me a ton of questions every day. She owned her own shift.

She took ownership of her journey. She knew what she wanted. And while she appreciated my opinion, she knew what she was capable of doing. She set and met her goals much quicker because of it. She is now a successful HR leader in education.

When you own your own shift, take ownership of your development, and define success for yourself, you will hold the key to your personal and professional fulfillment no matter where you work or how crazy things become around you.

DEFINING SUCCESS

You've done the work of Chapters 3 and 4 to understand your motivation, purpose, and values. Now, you have to do the work to define success in your terms and put it all together to determine what will create the meaningful, joyful work that will be such a big part of your life.

Define what success looks like for you and set your goals

before your organization does it for you. Do you want to be a CEO? Or is it your goal to be a frontline leader or an individual contributor who has some responsibility but still gets home for dinner and has weekends off?

Success may look like a bigger title and a bigger paycheck, or success for you may include leadership. The important thing for you to remember is that if you don't define your own path, the world will be happy to do it for you. And you have far too much to offer the world to fall in line and live out someone else's definition of success.

Real success is the culmination of things that brings you the most joy, uses your strengths, aligns with your values, serves your greater purpose, and allows you to do something meaningful. If you want to be truly fulfilled, define success for yourself in a way that capitalizes on all of those things. Let it evolve.

MAPPING IT OUT

Once you know where you want to go, you can map out the steps you need to take to get there. Consider where you are now and what skills or experiences you will need to move you in the direction you want to go. You can find job descriptions online and analyze the skills and experience required, but the best way to understand the role you're interested in growing into is to talk to someone who's doing it. Most people love to talk about what they do. Ask them how they prepared for the role, what they've discovered along the way, and what they wish they had known when they started out. Really dive in and get as much information as you can.

If your organization offers it, let them create a development plan for you. Just keep in mind that most of the time, the plan they help you develop will be specific to your growth within that organization. If you're lucky, you work with one of the more forward-thinking companies that are beginning to help employees build personal development plans to help them reach their goals—even if their plans ultimately take them away from the organization.

Or, if you're building your own plan, you can do whatever makes sense to you. It doesn't have to be anything formal. You can jot down ideas on a cocktail napkin or diagram everything out in fine detail. I'm a sucker for a whiteboard and dry-erase markers, so that's where my big picture goals and plans land. It doesn't matter how you record it; the value is in the process of setting the goal and getting clear on the steps you'll need to take. Careful not to get stuck here, though; goals are nice, but action is the only thing that will actually get you where you're going.

USING FEEDBACK AND ASSESSMENTS

Getting clear on your strengths and weaknesses is another big step you can take in this process. Seek out feedback about your performance. Ask questions about how you're doing. Learn how others view your strengths and where they might see opportunities for your growth. Don't wait for an annual evaluation. Get real-time feedback that you can use now.

Assessments can also help you focus in on your strengths and weaknesses. But do not get hung up on assessments; rather, use them as a place to get started. If you're still in college you likely have access to some useful assessments, so check with your career or resource center. If you're already working, check with your HR department to see if they have something to offer you. And if you're on your own then you can certainly find a number of options online. Just make sure they're reputable and assess what you're most interested in learning about yourself. There are lots of options out there.

Just promise me you won't let any assessment define or discourage you. Assessments are generally based on collective data—and whether that collective is one hundred or one million, you are the only you.

Whatever you choose to try, don't freak out over your weaknesses. You aren't perfect, no matter what your mama told you. None of us are. Simply get familiar with areas that are more challenging for you and use that knowledge to identify resources or people who will help you as you progress.

TOUGH-LOVE QUESTIONS

NEW OR ASPIRING LEADER

- What does success look like for you personally and professionally? Describe it with as much detail as possible.

EXPERIENCED LEADER

- Has your definition of success evolved since you began your leadership journey?
- How do you define success today?

CHAPTER 6

LOVING LEADERSHIP IN ACTION

Well, you're still reading. Or skimming, which is totally cool. (You're busy. I get it.) Either way, I have to assume that you're still interested in pursuing or continuing to pursue this leadership gig. If you've spent time considering the tough-love questions then you've likely made some real progress toward understanding your own "why," delved into who you want to be as a leader, and considered how you can take ownership for your own development and engagement. When people ask me what advice I would give a new leader, I often give the same answer. Beware conformity, stay curious, and seek courage over confidence.

BEWARE CONFORMITY

Richard was a senior level executive in an organization I worked with. He was smart, friendly, funny, and genuine, a super-cool guy. When I was in Richard's office one day, I noticed that he had only three personal items on his massive cherry wood desk: a picture of his wife and daughters, an autographed football, and a framed photo of a house.

The house in the picture was startling in its shabbiness. I saw broken windows, a door barely hanging on by the hinges, peeling paint, and a wire fence with a broken gate. "Is that your dream home? Something to keep you inspired?" I joked. He said, "Actually, that's the house I grew up in. I keep it there to keep me humble and remind myself who I really am."

Interested, I asked him to tell me more. He looked at me and said, "Well, I forgot who I was for a minute. And that picture helps me remember my truth. The truth is that I'm just a poor kid from the *other* side of town. A kid who worked my ass off to get as far away from the poverty and stigma of that house as possible. I put myself through college, worked hard for every single grade, and earned the best internships. And it paid off. I got great job offers and started climbing that ladder fast.

When I first started out in leadership, I was terrified that all those successful people I worked with were going to figure out I wasn't one of them. Like growing up poor in *that* neighborhood disqualified me somehow. I know it sounds stupid now but I didn't want to do anything that gave them the impression I didn't belong. I did everything I could to blend in. I wanted to make sure I walked the same, talked the same, and generally behaved the same as everyone else at the table. I couldn't be a different color, but I could sure as hell wear a nice suit and get rid of my accent."

Richard explained how he learned to play golf and order the right coffee at breakfast and the best wine at dinner. He worked very hard at transforming himself to be like the people he most wanted to impress.

One night, on the drive home after dinner with his colleagues and their spouses, Richard's wife made a comment that rattled him.

"Does that tie you wear ever feel a little *too* tight?" she asked.

She said it playfully, but Richard knew there was more to it. He asked her to explain.

"Well," she said, "work Richard is just really different than real Richard. It's not bad or anything, you just don't seem to be yourself around them. I understand work is work but it almost feels like you're holding your breath the entire time they're around."

Although she wasn't exactly being negative, her comment hit a nerve. Richard reflected on how he got where he was and asked himself some hard questions about how he wanted to show up in the world. He knew he wanted to set an example for his two daughters. He wanted them to know they could be themselves and still be successful.

Richard told me, "I realized I had worked really hard to do this work I love and have a life I'm proud of. But I had been working even harder to conform, to fit in, and be someone that wasn't totally me. And that was something I couldn't be proud of."

The picture of his childhood home served to remind him that he was both a scrappy, hard-working kid from the other side of town *and* a successful businessman. It reminded him to stay humble and most importantly to truly be himself, no matter how much pressure there may be to conform.

Conformity is the tendency to change or align our behaviors to match those around us in order to fit in. Conformity is a powerful social force. I mean you remember high school, right? If you ever used the argument "everybody else is doing it" to justify wearing neon parachute pants or a banana clip, then you already understand conformity. (If you didn't grow up in the fashion catastrophe that was the 80s, look it up, but please withhold judgment.)

If high school isn't proof enough of the power of conformity, then consider this: psychologists have found that most of us will go along with group opinion even when we know the answer is wrong. Consider the participants in an experiment by psychologist Solomon Asch.[36] They were asked to compare a line drawn on a sheet of paper to a set of three lines on another sheet. Their task was to choose the line from that set that matched the original. Pretty easy, right? Individually, it was; working alone, participants chose the correct match 98 percent of the time. But when they were placed in a group of three or more actors who intentionally selected the wrong line, 75 percent of participants went along with the group's obviously wrong answer at least once.

Social conformity is so powerful, we'll dismiss reality just to fit in! That means you're going to run into a lot of it, especially in the workplace. Every workplace. Yes, every one.

---

[36] Kendra Cherry, "The Ash Conformity Experiments: Asch's Seminal Experiments Demonstrated the Power of Conformity," *VerywellMind*, March 16, 2019, https://www.verywellmind.com/the-asch-conformity-experiments-2794996.

Many company leaders have insisted to me that their company is the exception. They're *different*. Why don't they have issues with conformity? Because they value the whole person and promote radical transparency and honesty in the workplace, they tell me. In fact, they say they are so very committed to their unique culture that they screen all interview candidates for culture fit first and skill fit second. After all, their culture simply isn't for everyone. (Anybody else see the creative conformity there?)

The truth is that even the most "out-of-the-box," culture-promoting companies have a box—it may be a different color box, but it's still a box. They may have different ideals and values and priorities, but you still have to fit in to get in. That's conformity.

While pressures to conform are something we all experience, it can be especially challenging for women and minorities working their way up. In her book, Sylvia Ann Hewlett cites research her group conducted that found 41 percent of "professionals of color said they had felt the need to compromise their authenticity in order to conform."[37] I've seen the struggle dozens of leaders of every color, gender, and sexual orientation have faced over the years. Sadly, many of these uniquely talented, cool-as-

---

[37] Sylvia Ann Hewlett, *Executive Presence: The Missing Link Between Merit and Success* (New York: Harper Business, 2014).

hell personalities had to leave some of the best parts of themselves at home each workday to blend in at work.

You might think leaders had more leeway to behave authentically at work, but sometimes, the opposite is true. I worked with a Hispanic CEO for several years, and I thought I knew him pretty well until a work dinner at a Mexican food restaurant. Our waiter struggled a bit with English so our CEO started speaking to him in Spanish. All eight of us at the table were totally surprised. In three years of working with this guy none of us knew he could speak Spanish!

I asked him later how it could be that none us knew that about him after working so closely together for so long. What he said shocked me even more. He confided, "No one wants to hear that from me, especially my leadership. They need to see me as simply a more tan version of themselves and *they* don't speak Spanish." I hated hearing it, but I knew what he was saying was true. As a female who has been the only one at the table several times in my career, I understood.

JUST BE YOURSELF?

Is there room in the workplace for you to be uniquely you? Many leadership experts say there is; in fact, they say it's essential. Authenticity—the ability to show up honestly and genuinely as yourself—is one of the qualities of great leadership that often makes the "top 10" list.

While I wholeheartedly believe in the value of being true to yourself, the reality is that the workplace is made up of dozens, hundreds, or even thousands of unique people. Can you imagine if we all brought our eccentricities to work? I mean, I was a human resource leader, policy policewoman, compliance keeper, and rule-maker while at the same time being a person with a penchant for colorful language, as you may have noticed. Obviously, I couldn't openly curse when performing my job duties. (Except that unfortunate department meeting incident for which I was appropriately reprimanded.)

In the workplace, a certain level of conformity is necessary. There are rules we agree to follow when we enter into an employment agreement. Some of those rules require us to moderate some of our behaviors, such as cursing, to help the group coexist and move together harmoniously and respectfully. Those rules are usually pretty clear and generally accepted. Those rules aren't typically the problem. Healthy conformity can be beneficial and even comforting. I mean it's nice to know that most people will stay in their own lane on the highway and not cut in line at the grocery store.

Problems crop up when there are unspoken pressures

and expectations about how you must behave to fit in, be accepted by the group, or gain career traction. In Richard's case those pressures led him to lose his accent and hide his story. In your case, you might feel pressure to regularly attend happy hours with the team, hold certain political views or values, or to dress and speak a certain way. Unhealthy conformity occurs when you try to meet these expectations in spite of the fact that you don't drink, passionately hold differing opinions, or despise tying a knot around your neck five days a week. Unhealthy conformity destroys individuality and creativity while chipping away at your confidence and authenticity and leads to...you guessed it...disengagement. Two of the top ten drivers of disengagement, in fact, are related to personal expression and the inability to express new or differing individual ideas and opinions.[38]

The pressure to conform in the workplace is especially intense if you have aspirations of climbing the ladder. Each rung of the ladder brings more exposure and closer scrutiny of practically everything you do, along with increasing pressure from the people holding your next promotion or pay increase in their hands. Their grip can get as tight, for you, as that tie you didn't want to wear around your neck. To get what you want, you can probably hold your breath and conform for a little while, but the

---

[38] "What Causes Employee Disengagement?" *Custom Insight*, https://www.custominsight.com/employee-engagement-survey/research-employee-disengagement.asp.

human spirit is a pretty powerful force too. And if you're putting on a different personality when you put on that suit, you're going to suffer, and that suffering will show up as disengagement in every area of your life, including your leadership.

As a leader you'll set the tone for the people reporting to you. People want to follow someone they can trust, so you need to show some of your authentic self. At other times, you will need to conform. Going too far either way sets a poor example. As a leader, you are going to want—and need—people around you who are creative, willing to innovate and challenge the status quo, *and* get along with others in a work setting.

As Sylvia Ann Hewlett wrote, "There's real tension between authenticity and conformity. How much to stand out, how much to fit in. I'm deeply aware of the value of not losing your identity, not losing what makes you unique. But you do need to do some balancing of authenticity and conformity."

It would be completely naïve and irresponsible for me to simply suggest that you just be yourself at work. What I will suggest is that you be keenly aware of conformity in your life and especially the workplace. Acknowledge that it exists and consider how it impacts the way you show up, speak up, and contribute. Are you hiding or holding back core parts of who you are to meet expectations, real or perceived, of others to belong or to fit in? How is conformity in the workplace impacting your ability to engage, to be and to bring your best to your work?

If you want to be like everybody else because you've found your place and your people, then rock it! But if you want to be like everybody else just to "fit in," then you may want to go ahead and start setting some money away for the therapy, coaching, and other self-help that may very well be in your future.

STAY CURIOUS

Albert Einstein once said, "I have no special talent. I am only passionately curious."

Curiosity is a natural human attribute responsible for practically every cool thing ever invented, built, or created. Defined as a desire to know, curiosity is the innate drive within you to explore, seek out information, and learn. It is the instinct that prompted you to master one of the most powerful words in existence shortly after learning to speak. That word? Why? It's the one-word question that you likely pestered your family, teachers, and grocery-store strangers with because you simply had to know the things you sensed you did not know. Important things like why is the sky blue, why is water wet, or why does that woman have a skull and snake picture on her arm?

But how did you know as a child that there were things you didn't know? Why not simply accept that the sky is blue and water is wet and go on about your begging for sugary cereal and leave that nice lady alone?

Psychologists, scientists, and philosophers have pondered that same question for eons, though I was surprised, as I dove into curiosity, to find out how little research has been conducted on the topic compared to other areas of human behavior. It seems to be gaining traction in academia and pop psychology, though, and there is consensus about at least a couple of aspects of curiosity: it is generally accepted that curiosity is a function of evolution and that it comes with a ton of benefits, for you and for business.

For you, curiosity is linked to general psychological well-being, happiness, reduced anxiety, empathy for others, and improved relationships, learning, and memory.[39] Scientists have found that our brains actually release dopamine and other feel-good chemicals when we run into new things.[40]

---

[39] Emily Campbell, "Six Surprising Benefits of Curiosity," *Greater Good Magazine*, September 24, 2015, https://greatergood.berkeley.edu/article/item/six_surprising_benefits_of_curiosity.

[40] Adoree Durayappah-Harrison, "The Secret Benefits of a Curious Mind," *Psychology Today*, October 8, 2014, https://www.psychologytoday.com/us/blog/thriving101/201410/the-secret-benefits-curious-mind.

For business, curiosity is linked to a wide range of benefits, including fewer decision-making errors, increased innovation, reduced conflict, improved communication, and team performance among others. Francesca Gino, a behavioral scientist and professor at Harvard Business School who also studied conformity, was surprised to discover these benefits, writing that, "curiosity is much more important to an enterprise's performance than was previously thought."[41]

Curiosity is truly the greatest superpower hiding in plain sight. For leaders, in fact, curiosity may be the single most powerful, yet under-utilized, skill in the workplace. As Gino shares:

> ...cultivating [curiosity] at all levels helps leaders and their employees adapt to uncertain market conditions and external pressures: When our curiosity is triggered, we think more deeply and rationally about decisions and come up with more creative solutions. In addition, curiosity allows leaders to gain more respect from their followers and inspires employees to develop more trusting and more collaborative relationships with colleagues.

That's a lot of leadership bang for the question buck.

---

41 Francesca Gino, "The Business Case for Curiosity," *Harvard Business Review*, September-October 2018.

Fortunately, being curious typically comes so naturally to us that we don't even notice it. It's a superpower you already have complete mastery of. While being curious is a skill you can practice and improve, it is not something you need to be taught. You already know how to ask questions. But will you?

Unfortunately, Gino found that as natural and valuable as curiosity may be, it is often squashed or discouraged in the workplace. In one study, she assessed the curiosity level of two hundred fifty employees at the beginning of their employment and again after six months. All of them experienced a drop in curiosity by an average of more than 20 percent. "...People were under pressure to complete their work quickly, they had little time to ask questions about broad processes or overall goals." Personally, I was a little surprised the drop wasn't greater. I've seen hundreds of new hires start out full of enthusiasm and big ideas only to be immediately consumed with the pace of work, insecure leaders, or unhealthy organizational conformity.

It's really no surprise that remaining curious at work is such a challenge. The natural curiosity we're born with is discouraged from an early age. As children we are taught to do as we're told. Questioning authority is not allowed. First parents, then our teachers expect unquestioned compliance and reward it with leadership awards like the one my daughter received in kindergarten.

In elementary school, we can retain some of that curiosity. Sure, we are instructed to seek permission by raising our hand if we have a question or want to answer one. But young children are curious about everything and often have no concept of a stupid question or being wrong. Asking and answering questions is exciting when we're young.

But by the time we get to middle school and high school, raising our hand to ask or answer a question in a room full of our peers turns into a risky venture that may result in social embarrassment, which is akin to death for a teenager. A person only has to experience the pain of asking a "stupid" question or being shamed, even if unintentionally, a few times before they stop asking questions. And heaven forbid you raise your hand to *answer* a question and get it wrong. I can feel my neck and ears getting red just thinking about the horror of it.

Those lessons have staying power. I've often had new leaders share that they are simply not comfortable asking questions in meetings or in the presence of more experienced or senior leaders because they don't want to look stupid. So even when employees are able to overcome the challenges of remaining curious, asking questions at work can be difficult.

QUESTION EVERYTHING

The thing is, you have to keep asking questions. As the Chinese proverb states, "He who asks is a fool for five minutes, he who does not ask is a fool forever." Genuine curiosity can serve you in so many ways when it comes to work. Questions can diffuse arguments, establish connections, and convey empathy with other people. Being curious can help you to stay humble, be approachable, and avoid imposing bias or judgment on others. It can even reduce stress.

One of the greatest challenges that leaders face right now is the exponentially increasing rate of change. We've talked about it in previous chapters because it's a real issue for a lot of people in the workplace. When everything seems to be changing faster and uncertainty is the norm, curiosity is the key to both your personal sanity and your leadership success.

One reason is that it's hard to be curious and stressed out at the same time. Though it is possible. Ever watch a scary movie while peering through loosely laced fingers? You're simultaneously freaked out about what's going on and really curious about what's going to happen next. Leaders often feel this way; with so many things happening at once, it can feel like you have no control at all. And sometimes you don't. But what you do have control of is the way you approach and manage every situation.

When you choose to be curious and make a habit of asking questions instead of making judgments or assumptions, you'll gain perspective that's not available when looking for the "right" answer. You'll be able to see and evaluate a situation as it is and move others through seemingly impossible situations simply by being curious.

Even better, when you approach challenging situations with curiosity, you give your peers and teams permission to do the same thing. You create a safe space for questioning the status quo and creative, out-of-the-box thinking that generates more possibilities than barriers to solving problems. You quite literally exchange stress and dread for excitement and possibility.

As I mentioned before, you already know how to ask questions. If you've forgotten, simply ask Why, What if, and How. Don't want to sound like a jerk? You can use a phrase such as "Can you help me understand...?" Worried about sounding stupid? Try using the phrase, "I wonder..." This is a personal favorite as it feels more like mental exploration and deep thinking than an admission of ignorance.

I have been known to write the words "Question Everything" at the top of my office whiteboard as a reminder for me and everyone on my team to stay curious. To question processes, policies, decisions, and even me. I'll admit it's easier to write it on a white board than it is to practice. Challenging the status quo and asking questions at the risk of being thought a fool is tough. Allowing yourself to be challenged can be tougher. But loving leadership requires it. You can't possibly have all the answers or see all the angles—you're just one person. But if you practice curiosity and demonstrate it for your team, you'll give them permission to challenge what they see and ask the questions burning in their bellies. All that curiosity and exploration will drive the creativity and innovation that is critically necessary at work today. It takes courage to question everything.

COURAGE OVER CONFIDENCE

If you read even a single article or how-to book on leadership, there's a very strong chance that you'll be instructed to "be confident." You'll be informed that confidence is *the* top essential quality of great leadership. And you may be told things like "no confidence, no leadership," and my personal favorite "fake it 'till you make it." But what you may not hear is what exactly *it* is.

Well, according to Merriam-Webster:

> Confidence is a noun defined as a feeling or consciousness of one's powers; faith or belief that one will act in a right, proper, or effective way; and the quality or state of being certain.

> Confident is an adjective meaning full of conviction: certain; and having or showing assurance and self-reliance.

So being self-confident means believing in yourself, your decisions, or your actions *with certainty*. And confidence is the belief that you will *certainly* do the right thing, make the right decisions, and be effective. No pressure!

Of course confidence is an important quality in all areas of your life. Confidence is certainly an important quality when your job is to influence others. If you're a leader, people are looking to you for guidance, direction, and some level of certainty that you "will act in a right, proper, or effective way" while moving them in the right direction. The same way that you might expect your next-level leader to do. They will need to have enough confidence in you to follow you.

The thing is, though, that new job title or longer list of responsibilities doesn't come with a certificate of confidence and certainty. In fact, it probably exposes you to a lot of things you've never done before.

Self-confidence is largely established through past experiences. Your boss demonstrated confidence in you when they hired or promoted you into that leadership role. Confidence likely grounded in your past performance. And you're probably stepping up with a decent amount of self-confidence based on those same experiences. That's great, but guess what? Leadership is a whole new ball game. You're going to experience curveballs and screwballs (metaphorical and literal) like you've never seen before. There will be times that you'll expect a certain level of performance from yourself based on past experience; when something goes wrong, your confidence can take a hit.

Then you'll come to the office of someone like me, saying, "I'm not sure I can do this."

Or "I don't know if I'm the right person for this role."

Or "I feel like an idiot. I didn't think this would be so hard."

To which I most often reply;

"Of course it's hard. You've never done it before. You've never had this level of responsibility with this many people expecting this much of you. And the learning curve for new leaders is crazy steep in the beginning. You were probably really practiced and skilled at the role you held before; that's likely why you were promoted. But leadership is hard. Leading people from the middle is hard. You are learning to manage the expectations and needs of people looking to you for guidance while figuring out how to manage and meet the expectations of people above you.

You're developing new skills through new experiences. You're stretching and growing in ways similar to what you likely went through when learning your previous role. The difference with leadership is that there are a lot of eyes on you. There are also high expectations of you. From others, yes. But I bet you put plenty of pressure on yourself too. Pressure to meet those expectations of great leadership you read about. Pressure to prove that you deserve the leadership role. All that pressure can do a number on your confidence."

BE IT UNTIL YOU BELIEVE IT

"Fake it 'till you make it" is a phrase we hear a lot today, especially when it comes to confidence. It's a well-intended sentiment meant to help people visualize and ideate the characteristics they want to have and then actually imitate those behaviors, i.e., do it until it becomes comfortable. I'm not a fan of faking it.

As an alternative, I tell my clients to "be it until you believe it." The term "fake it" implies that you are doing something that isn't authentic or really you. And that's not true. You are, after all, the one doing it! Whether you're trying on a new skill, practicing a new behavior, or making a presentation while shaking in your shoes—you're doing it. You may be scared of failing nine different ways, being rejected, laughed at or a million other things your imagination can conjure up, but you're not "faking" anything. You simply aren't letting the fear take over, stop you, or show through. This is the definition of courage. Being afraid and doing it anyway!

Courage is the mental or moral strength to venture, persevere, and withstand in danger, fear, or difficulty.

Courage means you are afraid but you do it anyway. Confidence is what comes *after* you survive the experience.

Afraid you'll screw something up on that project working directly with the CEO? Do it anyway.

Afraid you'll say the wrong thing in a difficult conversation? Do it anyway.

Afraid to make the final staffing decision when every other leader is out of town? Do it anyway.

Obviously, in any of these situations, you need to prepare, gather information, ask questions, and be as informed as you can be, which is all any of us can ever really do. Courage and stupid may be close cousins but I'm assuming you understand the difference.

You can't have certainty without the experience, and you can't have the experience without the courage to show up and actually engage in the experience.

I know it's hard to do it anyway. It has been my experience in life and leadership that most of us want to be certain of the outcome before we actually do anything. We want to know that we'll be good at something before we'll try it. But you cannot possibly know if you're good at anything you haven't tried! You can have a pretty good idea based on past experiences and other things you've been really good at, but you cannot be certain until you do the thing! So back off of yourself! As a leader, you are going to have lots of opportunities to stretch and experience new things. If you're too busy "faking" confidence you might miss the fact that you are actually doing and growing. You'll discount the learning as pretending and miss giving yourself credit for the growth you've gained.

The one thing that I am most confident of, after coaching hundreds of leaders, is the fact that everyone wants to be more confident! But what you need more than confidence, the thing you have to have first, is courage. The courage to show up, to be vulnerable, and to learn. The courage to do what scares you. The courage to be it until you believe it.

Swap the pressure of confidence and certainty for courage and experience. Courage doesn't require you to know or be certain. Courage simply asks that you show up and be willing. Have the courage to step up to the challenge, whatever it may be, certain ONLY of the fact that you will gain experience and learn something no matter the outcome.

Do the things and learn the stuff and I promise the confidence will follow.

TOUGH-LOVE QUESTIONS
NEW OR ASPIRING LEADER

- Is a lack of confidence holding you back in any area of your work?
- What steps would you take in your career if you swapped confidence for courage and did it anyway?

EXPERIENCED LEADER

- Where are you faking it?
- Are there areas in your leadership or your life where conformity has taken over?
- How can you begin to bring more of your real self into those areas?

CONCLUSION

WHAT'S LOVE GOT TO DO WITH IT?

If you're reading this page and you've done the work in this book, congratulations! You are already miles ahead of the curve. You have done more than most people, let alone leaders, ever do for themselves. You know yourself, and what you want, better than ever.

No matter what you've been told about leadership as a kindergarten student or as CEO of a Fortune 500 company, the truth is that real leadership is hard and it is not for everyone. Leaders have real impact on real people in our organizations, our communities, and our homes. The fact that it's hard and so impactful means that leadership is not something to pursue without some meaningful measure of personal consideration. You've done that.

I wrote this book to help you determine if leadership is right for you. And maybe you've decided it's not. That's great! Now that you know that, you can avoid taking on a role or following a career path that doesn't serve you or those around you. Instead, you are free to pursue other work that lights you up and allows you to be your best, like Amanda, the nurse who returned to her first love—caring for patients one-on-one. That's important work too.

This is why I say love it or leave it. I mean it. If it's right for you, kick ass. If it's not, then figure out what lights you up and kick ass at that—sans suffering.

If you have decided that leadership is right for you—that it serves a purpose in your life that you connect with on a greater scale—that's great too! The world needs more leaders that *choose* leadership. Connecting with leadership on a meaningful level that aligns with your personal values, means that you can bring joy *and* love to the role. I know, just saying it that way is giving me a cavity, it's so sugary sweet. But it's true! You are now positioned to positively impact and empower others in a real way. To be a good leader that real people, with real lives—will gladly follow.

You are no longer the average leader. You have done some really personal work to make sure you're able to stay grounded even in the midst of massive restructure.

You have accepted that leadership is challenging because it's not only important to the organization, it's important to you. You're able to plug into your own purpose and motivation when your boss's "leadership spirit animal" is a rabid squirrel and even when you get a new boss every couple of years. You understand the importance of alignment between values and actions. And you appreciate that this is important, not only for you, but also for everyone around you. You engage because you've decided that your work, your purpose, your role, and your impact are meaningful to you, personally *and* professionally.

You may not always feel like giving 110 percent, but you'll show up, give your best, and leave people and places a little better for you having been present. You see change for what it is—growth, learning, and sometimes adventure. You appreciate that it can be exhausting and challenging but you recognize that it isn't personal, it just is. And when there are hard choices to make you're going to approach them with courage and curiosity.

LOVING LEADERSHIP

Loving leadership is not a euphemism for being a "great" leader. Throughout this book we've talked a lot about you, how you feel about yourself, and what you define as your core values. That's because our love of ourselves shows up in everything we do—including work. You've got to love this leadership thing. You have to know in your soul that guiding and influencing the success of others is something that you value. If leadership is an intrinsically rewarding part of your life, then it's time to rock 'n roll with awareness and love, creating a positive impact wherever you are.

A PERSONAL NOTE

I wrote this book because I had to. Whether we talk about it or not, suffering in the workplace is real. Today we call it disengagement or burnout, and tomorrow we'll call it experience or something else. The reality is that too many people are doing what they think they should do, chasing someone else's idea of success and assuming that misery is just part of the deal. It doesn't have to be!

The most important element in your journey is *you*. When you show up each day as a self-aware, intentional human and you love the work you do, you *will* experience and create joy. I've seen it happen time and again. My personal hope for you is that you will bring your whole, creative, purpose-filled, bad-ass self to your work—whatever you choose to do.

I wrote this book *for* you because this is your journey. And as far as we know you only get one. It's up to you to define success for yourself and decide if serving others through leadership serves you on your one journey. The world is happy to insist that leadership equals success. But each day that you rise for "work" you will face your own reflection in the mirror. Ask yourself, do I love what I'm doing? Am I having an impact and serving a purpose that I'm proud of?

I wrote this book *about* you because once you decide that leadership is the right path for you, most things very quickly cease to be about you at all. The training you receive will be about making you more effective, productive, and all kinds of great for the company. You'll be taught, groomed, and instructed to serve—the business, the mission, the people. You'll be blasted with "how to" and "must haves." Don't lose yourself in all the training and expectations. What foundationally makes you a truly good leader comes from within you. Build on that.

I also wrote this book for the people that you may have the opportunity to impact. Every decision you make, every word you say, every bit of encouragement you share, or don't, will directly affect another human being. Human beings who need you to choose for yourself and decide if leadership is right for you. Human beings who need you to love the responsibility, the influence, and the impact of leadership. Human beings who need you to love it or leave it.

ACKNOWLEDGMENTS

Leadership is hard and HR leadership may be just a tad harder.

This book is the product of twenty years of experience in a field that I truly felt called to—human resources. Experience that has been as exciting and fulfilling as it has been frustrating. I've had the opportunity to help open new hospitals, launch new technologies, and participate in complete industry transformations. But the greatest privilege has been supporting the human beings I've worked with at every stage of the journey.

I learned the most from the people who trusted me with their stories, their successes, their frustrations, and their suffering—both personal and professional. I've been trusted with the most exciting news and the most devastating details. I've helped onboard and layoff. I've helped people rebuild after natural disasters and recover from the walking, talking disasters. I've celebrated with the accomplished and consoled the grieving. I am grateful for every person and every single experience.

I've also screwed up as much as I've gotten right. I've made lifelong friends, and I've pissed people off—both are part of life, learning and being in HR. However, I regret those situations where my learning may have come at the expense of any other human being. Hindsight can be a little crappy in its perfection.

***

This book and so many other accomplishments in my life would never have happened without the unconditional love and encouragement of my grandmother, the late saint, Marie Noel. Your faith in me transcended every trauma, and your faith in God saved us all. So how does it look from up there, Granny?

Misty Brown, Cindy Noel and John Michael Grant—my sisters and my little brother—you are walking, talking miracles and I am so proud of you. We survived, we overcame, and we're just getting started. Thank you for loving me. I love you.

Douglas Cagle, you listen, listen, and listen some more. Thank you for encouraging all of my big ideas over the years, especially this book. You keep me grounded and give me a safe place to freak out occasionally. Thank you for being my leader guinea pig. You are loving leadership personified. Your empathy, compassion, and heart for healthcare leadership is truly inspiring.

Dr. Bradley Mayer, Cary Erickson, Jennifer Barroeta, Debbie Frazier, Stephanie Flory, and Sandra Prudhomme from whom I learned so very much. I fell in love with HR because you were so freaking good at it. You inspired me, you encouraged me, and you even put up with me when I knew it all. Thank you for believing in me when I struggled to believe in myself.

Craig Desmond and Dr. Jeffery Canose—You indulged and encouraged my interests in operations. You allowed me to truly be myself and to be, as one of you put it, "*not your typical HR leader!*" You each brought such passion to the business of healing and I learned so much from you. Thank you.

Michelle Adams, my sister-friend. There are no words to express how much your friendship has meant to me all these years. I've never laughed so much, cried so hard, or nearly died so many times as I have with you. We've been through it all—and you never let me forget that I can do whatever I set my mind to do. Thank you for your encouragement. Thank you for your friendship. I love you, sister.

A special note of gratitude to Michelene Moody. My career started the day you offered me a job. The first professional, female role model I'd ever had—I learned everything I really needed to know about strong leadership from you. You took me in when I didn't know who I was or who I wanted to be. I am so grateful to you, Celeste, and your family.

All right universe—I wrote the damn book! Now what?

ABOUT THE AUTHOR

ANGIE NOEL wants to change the way we talk about leadership. As an HR executive, she spent twenty years supporting hundreds of leaders—frontline to CEO—many struggling with stress, frustration, and self-doubt. After overcoming her own burnout and disengagement, Angie committed to helping others avoid that suffering by getting candid about the unspoken challenges of leadership. A sought-after speaker and coach known for her human behavior expertise, extreme motivation, and tough love, Angie inspires clients and audiences to take control of their leadership journey to achieve professional success *and* personal fulfillment. Angie is the Founder and CEO of Leading With Mission, and lives in Texas. Learn more at angienoel.com.

Made in the USA
San Bernardino, CA
11 July 2020